NEW YORK NEW JERSEY

A Vignette of the Metropolitan Region

George W. Carey

A Vignette of the
New York—New
Jersey Metropolitan
Region

Association of American Geographers

Comparative Metropolitan Analysis Project

Vol. 1   Contemporary Metropolitan America: Twenty Geographical Vignettes.
         Cambridge: Ballinger Publishing Company, 1976.
Vol. 2. Urban Policymaking and Metropolitan Dynamics: A Comparative Geo-
         graphical Analysis. Cambridge: Ballinger Publishing Company, 1976.
Vol. 3. A Comparative Atlas of America's Great Cities: Twenty Metropolitan
         Regions. Minneapolis: University of Minnesota Press, 1976.

Vignettes of the following metropolitan regions are also published by Ballinger
Publishing Company as separate monographs:

- Boston
- New York-New Jersey
- Philadelphia
- Hartford-Central Connecticut
- Baltimore
- New Orleans

- Chicago
- St. Paul-Minneapolis
- Seattle
- Miami
- Los Angeles

Research Director:
John S. Adams, University of Minnesota

Associate Director and Atlas Editor:
Ronald Abler, Pennsylvania State University

Chief Cartographer:
Ki–Suk Lee, University of Minnesota

Steering Committee and Editorial Board:
Brian J.L. Berry, Chairman, University of Chicago
John R. Borchert, University of Minnesota
Frank E. Horton, Southern Illinois University
J. Warren Nystrom, Association of American Geographers
James E. Vance, Jr., University of California, Berkeley
David Ward, University of Wisconsin

Supported by a grant from the National Science Foundation.

A Vignette of the New York-New Jersey Metropolitan Region

George W. Carey
Rutgers University
Newark, New Jersey

Ballinger Publishing Company ● Cambridge, Massachusetts
A Subsidiary of J.B. Lippincott Company

This book is printed on recycled paper.

International Standard Book Number: 0-88410-436-2

Library of Congress Cataloging in Publication Data

Printed in the United States of America

Library of Congress Cataloging in Publication Data

Carey, George Warren, 1927–
   A vignette of the New York–New Jersey metropolitan region.

   Bibliography: p.
   1. New York metropolitan area—Social conditions. 2. New York metropolitan
area—Economic conditions. 3. Housing—New York metropolitan area. I. Title.
HN80.N5C37   309.1'747'104   76-4796
ISBN 0-88410-436-2

Contents

List of Figures

List of Tables

Preface

In preparing this study for the Comparative Metropolitan Analysis Project, I have tried to present a regional description of the urbanized core of the New York–New Jersey metropolis in a manner which avoids the penalties of scholarly writing as much as possible, and which anchors itself in field experience as much as possible. Since all of the ideas in this monograph did not spring full blown from my brow, I wish to call attention to the bibliographical notes at the conclusion in which those publications to which I am chiefly indebted are listed.

Paramount among these sources are the two great New York Metropolitan Regional Studies sponsored by the Regional Plan Association—one of the 1930s and the other of the 1950s. Indispensable to the serious field trip devotee in the region are the Hagstrom Company's maps and atlases, the WPA *New York City Guide* of 1930s, and the AIA Guide to New York City of the 1960s.

In the area of New York City and Newark housing policy, my colleagues at Rutgers—George Sternlieb and Jim Hughes—are sources of information of the highest order. I owe many of my insights in the area of environmental quality to my teacher, colleague, and friend Leonard Zobler, of Barnard College, Columbia University, and to my Rutger associates Michael Greenberg and Robert Hordon.

My eyes were opened to the landscape of Paterson, New Jersey, when Sally Gibson of the Paterson Museum took me on a walking tour which is the basis for much of the Paterson section of this study and which was developed by the Great Falls Development Corporation.

Many acute observers have accompanied me on various field trips which I have led in the region. They have enriched my understanding more than they, perhaps, realize: Maurice Yeates, Barry Garner, David Lownethal, Peirce Lewis, Mile Woldenberg, Art Getis, Robert Harper, Ted Schmudde, Briavel Holcomb, and most of the Rutgers geographers come to mind. Their material is reflected in both the text and photographs.

Many thanks to John S. Adams and Ron Abler who made it possible for me to participate in the project. Ron Foresta, who served as a research aide when the pressures got tough, deserves my appreciation, as do my other colleagues, friends, and students in the Urban Studies subculture at Rutgers. I look back on this task with misgivings and unease at the audacity implicit in presuming to prepare a study of such a metropolitan giant in so few pages.

And so I emphasize that all of the overgeneralizations, gaffes, and canards which may be found in this work are mine alone.

Tappan, New York 1974

A Vignette of the
New York—New
Jersey Metropolitan
Region

An Overview of the Region

The area known as the New York Metropolitan Region (NYMR) extends over those portions of three states which adjoin where the waters of the Hudson and the Raritan rivers mingle with those of the Atlantic Ocean, Long Island Sound, and the numerous bays, channels, and kills of the port of New York and New Jersey (Figure 1). Connecticut on the mainland to the East; New York in the center, extending over the vast expanse of Long Island; and New Jersey on the mainland to the west are the major political jurisdictions.

Twenty-two counties are roughly included within this metropolitan giant—one in Connecticut, nine in New Jersey, twelve in New York. The focal point of the region is New York City, located upon a group of islands at the junction of the principal bodies of water. Of the five counties in New York City only one—the Bronx—is principally on the mainland. Kings County (Brooklyn) and Queens County are on the western end of Long Island, Richmond County is on Staten Island, and most of New York County is on Manhattan Island.

As the map reveals, the rolling terrain of the coastal plain covers most of New York City, but the mainland to the northwest is quite broken. The "mountains" alluded to rarely exceed 800 feet in elevation, but the relief is usually sharply defined and numerous cliff faces and escarpments are present which have slowed urbanization to the northwest and channeled it to the northeast, east, and southwest.

To some extent areas such as the Ramapo and Putnam mountains will remain permanent-

ly undeveloped. Harriman State Park, Bear Mountain State Park, and the United States Military Reservation at West Point are all located in the Ramapo subregion, while major portions of Putnam County are held in forested watershed lands.

Nevertheless, major arteries have penetrated these barriers and Orange County in the trans-Ramapo area is in development as is Dutchess County to the north of the Putname Mountains. The New York State Thruway found its way from New York City upstate through the pass at Suffern on the Ramapo River that had formerly been used by Indian trails, corduroy roads, railroads, and U.S. Route 17. Major routes like U.S. 9 and the Taconic State Parkway have sliced northward through the difficult terrain of the Putnam Mountains to Dutchess County, incorporating the environs of Poughkeepsie in the metropolitan system.

In New Jersey to the west, core cities like Elizabeth, Newark, and Jersey City lie in the zone between the Watchung Mountains and the tidewater. Paterson, New Jersey, another old core city, lies at the fall line where the Passaic River drops over the Watchungs in Passaic Falls. Railroads and highways have bypassed or cut through the Watchungs. The land behind them is in middevelopment today.

It was not until the 1930s when the beautiful George Washington Bridge was completed spanning the Hudson River between Manhattan and New Jersey that the barrier of the Palisades was effectively breached. Since then, the area between back slopes of the cliffs and the Ram-

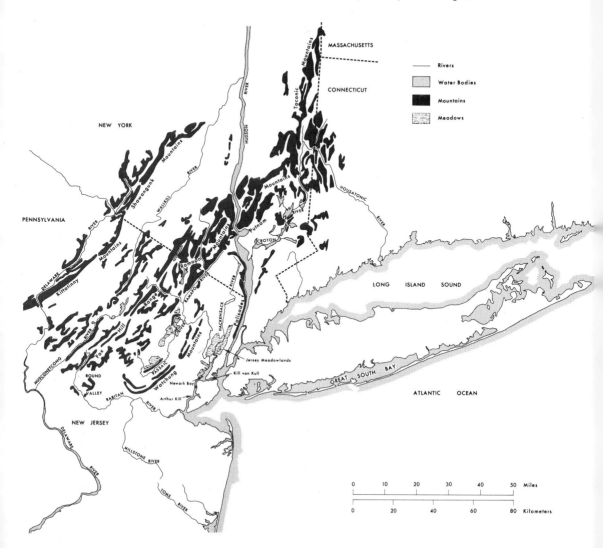

Figure 1.   Major Natural Features of the New York Metropolitan Region (NYMR)

apo River has become extensively urbanized. Bergen County, New Jersey, and Rockland County, New York lie within this zone. The Rockland County portion, which lagged in development at first, has experienced extremely rapid growth since the New York State Thruway Bridge provided a Hudson River crossing in the 1950s. It penetrates the Palisades at Nyack.

To the East, in Connecticut, the region has grown up around other old core cities on the coastal plain like Bridgeport. The easy terrain in this direction and also to the Southwest has led to the development of a corridor of trans-

portation facilities which reaches from Boston to the national capital, with the NYMR roughly at the center.

The still easier terrain of Long Island, to the East, has provided even less impediment to development. The remarkable photograph in Figure 2 presents a vista along the entire 120 mile length of this suburb. Brooklyn and Queens, on the near tip of the island, are the heart of New York City. Beyond, the heavily urbanized zone of Nassau County blends into the outer reaches of Suffolk County where suburbs, rural spaces, and a seashore resort industry coexist in an unstable relationship.

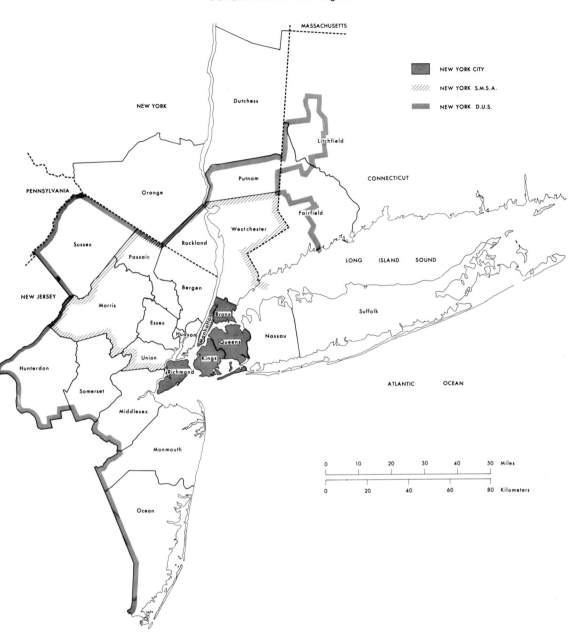

Figure 3. New York Metropolitan Region Counties.

regional patterns which we have been discussing provide minor eddies around these nuclei.

Many suburban residents make a daily journey to work in the suburbs rather than the central city. Moreover, increasing numbers of core city residents are journeying to work in the suburbs rather than the city. Thus, in order to understand the location of economic activity in the NYMR, we must understand something of the industrial parks, office buildings, warehousing facilities, wholesaling centers, and retailing hubs in the suburbs as well as the center city. Port Newark-Elizabeth and Paramus in New Jersey, and Nassau and Dutchess (headquarters for IBM operations) counties in

New York assume their importance alongside Manhattan.

Finally, in those portions of this study which do concentrate upon New York City, the prognosis will be mixed. Even with respect to activities which retain some vitality there, standardized operations which are routine and require a large labor force are suburbanizing. These fields include advertising and the media, central office functions of major coporations, the fashion industry, publishing, finance and insurance, the securities industry, international trade, and rare and specialized forms of retailing which command a far-flung market. It seems likely that the Manhattan office building boom of the past twenty-five years has come to a close. Many vacancies go unfilled in the towers of Wall Street as a result of what has probably been an overbuilding of office space. To a certain extent government has stepped in as a kind of "tenant of last resort." Major state and federal bureaus and departments have located in Wall Street space, helping to stabilize it. But clearly even in the areas of finance, insurance, real estate, and business services, New York City is no longer the whole story. Indeed, even within New York City, the undeniably great strength still left in these sectors lies concentrated in Manhattan south of 70th Street. Secondary centers like Brooklyn and Newark are eroding.

In line with this discussion, this overview of the NYMR will possibly be more decentralized from a focus on Manhattan than the reader may anticipate. Yet from the standpoint of what some writers are calling a massive economic "disinvestment" in the core city counties it may well prove to be not suburbanized enough.

The New York Metropolitan Region—Process, Form, and Control

PROCESS

The essence of the New York Metropolitan Region (NYMR) is that its hinterland of reference is the world. Jean Gottmann has pointed out that the NYMR and its contiguous urbanized area—more than any other American city region—serves as a hinge between the United States and the rest of the world—the vital junction between the variegated commodity and service flows which originate within the immense productive network formed by United States industry and comparably scaled foreign productive behemoths such as the European Economic Community and Japan, among others.

American society depends for its existence upon the flow of goods and services from the cities where they are produced to the destinations where they are consumed. An elaborate socioeconomic system has developed whereby, for instance, primary materials flow from mines, farmlands, forests, and oceans to staging points where they are converted into intermediate or final products for consumption. At these staging points—by other routes—energy, labor, and capital resources are accumulated to facilitate the process of production and ancillary activities arise to sustain the lifestyle of the population who are there engaged in the complex human relationships of production.

The multibranched network of rivers, roads, railroads, pipelines, shipping lanes, power lines, telephone and telegraph cables, airline routes, and other channels over which this

immense complexity of flow passes constitutes the veritable circulatory and nervous system of our society. The staging points, or sites of production, which lie at the major nodes where these channels intersect are critical elements of human settlements—villages, towns, cities, metropolises.

Some small towns and cities serve as productive and distributive nodes for the limited area which constitutes their hinterland. These are smaller in scale than their larger siblings which relate to regions which are national or subnational in scope.

William Warntz has worked out an elaborate statistical measurement which he calls "income potential," measuring the intensity of personal income at various points on the earth's surface (Figure 4). Dumbell-shaped contours of enormous income potential ring the NYMR, on the one hand, and the Rhine delta seaports of the European Economic Community, on the other. If we imagine these points to resemble magnetic poles, and if we were able on a world scale to duplicate the high school physics experiment of sprinkling iron filings on the earth's surface between the magnetic poles, it becomes possible to image the discipline with which the filings would slowly flow toward these poles as the map is tapped. If each filing were a ship, the metaphor would be complete.

The visitor to New York has only to stand on the eastern shore of Staten Island, in Van Briesen Park, on a sunny Wednesday (when visibility is good, and the midweek maritime traffic is at its peak) to see the magnet meta-

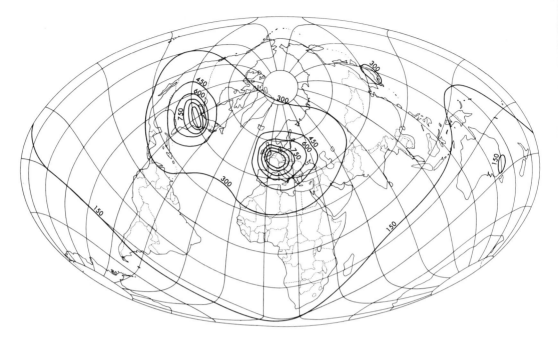

Figure 4. World Income Potentials about 1960. Source: William Warntz.

phor made concrete in the flow of container ships into and out of the harbor. And for each container ship (with perhaps 900 containers) a host of invisible flows—of messages, information, orders, insurance and financial arrangements—passes through the air or through cables invisible to the eye to and from the port.

The essence of the NYMR is that it is the prime United States node for worldwide flows. But, at the regional or local scale, the resident has a more limited vision and his existence expresses itself in a small life space within the regional system. We face a challenging task—to come to grips with the grand scale of the major processes in the region, and yet to understand their relationship in numerous localities with the people who inhabit it and who view it with the perspective of the ant in a lawn. What is orderly at one scale, appears a chaotic thicket at another.

FORM

If the NYMR represents the node where important flows which sustain our society—and other societies—converge, this fact has a profound effect on the physical form which the

social organization of the region assumes. A parcel of land in a city is valuable depending upon that to which it gives access. If it is so located that it gives its user access to the array of goods, services, and opportunities passing through the NYMR, it will be more valuable than one remote from the metropolitan center. Since locations in the NYMR supply users with immediate access to more than 400 out of the 450 broad categories of American economic activity, and since the remaining fifty or so are easily available to the region, it follows that some of the region's real estate will be among the most valuable in the world.

This is true particularly at the traditional heart of the region—the island of Manhattan. This central subarea of the primate nodal region in the United States serves as the epitome of the city as conceived by Karl Deutsch:

> Any metropolis can be thought of as a huge engine of communication, a device to enlarge the range and reduce the cost of individual and social choices. In the familiar telephone switchboard, the choices consist of many different lines. Plugging in the wires to connect any two lines is an act of commitment, since it implies foregoing the making of other connections. The concentra-

tion of available outlets on the switchboard permits a wider range of alternative choices than would prevail under any more dispersed arrangement. The limits of the potentially useful size of a switchboard are fixed by the capacity of the type of switching and control equipment available.... The facilities of the metropolis for transport and communication are the equivalent of the switchboard (p. 96).

To amplify and enrich Deutsch's metaphor, consider a clay contoured model of the New York–New Jersey–Connecticut urbanized area, the height of which at any point is proportional to the intensity of business activity carried forward at that location (Figure 5). The towering twin peaks emerge on Manhattan, near the center of the pattern. The southernmost lies at the Wall Street financial complex. A saddle surface sags to a "pass" of relatively lower business activity near Canal Street. From there the surface climbs to the midtown Manhattan peak near 42nd Street, where a vast amount of central business office and retailing activities thrive in the shadow of the United Nations on the East River. On the sloping flanks of these peaks—northward into Harlem, across the East River in Brooklyn and Queens, and across the Harlem River into the Bronx—lie acre after acre of land devoted to apartment houses of varying age, condition, tenantry, and ownership.

Business intensity can also be represented by employment per acre in the NYMR (Figure 6). Yet as one gets farther from the intense activity of the Manhattan center, uses other than commercial may successfully bid for the cheaper land. In Brooklyn, for example, the high "ridge" along Atlantic and Fifth avenues in the west—a privileged position of access to Manhattan by six subway tunnels, one vehicular tunnel, three bridges, and four vertically superimposed layers of roadway running along the shore—rapidly slopes off into the vast residential areas of Bedford Stuyvesant, Bushwick, Flatbush, Williamsburg, and Brownsville. Since most of the 600,000-plus housing units for Brooklyn's more than two million people were built since 1901, this area represents one of the greatest construction efforts in human history. It was an effort which was fueled by the nineteenth century explosion of economic activity at the Manhattan center and which fed on the housing needs of the millions who were drawn to the city to provide labor, each wave of immigrant labor destined to dwell in tenement houses built by its predecessors.

Figure 5. Activity Model, New York Metropolitan Region. The height of the clay above the map conceptualizes human activities. The two-pronged summit is Manhattan (Wall Street and Midtown). Lower crests are Brooklyn (nearer) and urban New Jersey (farther). Source: Reproduced by permission of Thomas J. Thomas, who prepared the model for the Tri-State Transportation Commission.

As time has passed, seaport activity has shifted to New Jersey. In that segment of the NYMR major rail, airport, road, and pipeline facilities adjoin one another. Since large acreages of marshland lie between the transportation axis and Newark Bay, landfill efforts have been undertaken which have led to container port construction. This setting has been conducive to the design of facilities which are capable of transferring cargoes from one transportation mode to another with ease and despatch. So the greatness of New York as a seaport resides in Port Newark and Port Elizabeth—both in the state of New Jersey—while many of the once vaunted dock areas of Brooklyn and Manhattan rot into a rich flotsam which defies the efforts of the Coast Guard to clear it from the estuary.

The growth of this urban region has obviously long since spilled over the political boundaries of New York City, to engulf portions of three states, numerous counties, municipalities, and various other jurisdictions. Wood, in writing of this confusion of governmental complexity which defies rational planning and con-

Figure 6. Employment, Manhattan CBD. The height of the paper forms is proportional to employment density in Manhattan circa 1969. Each quadrant is forty acres. The total volume of jobs is two million. Source: Reproduced by permission of Ernst Hacker who prepared the model for the New York City Planning Commission.

trol in the region, entitled his book *1400 Governments* for good reason.

THE PROBLEM OF REGIONAL CONTROL—AN OUTLINE

At one extreme of scale in the NYMR are tiny, semiautonomous fire, sewer, and school tax districts whose boundaries do not always coincide with those of the municipalities which they serve. At the intermediate range of scale we find municipalities, towns, counties, and the five boroughs into which New York City is divided. At the other extreme of scale are the metropolitan giants—the Port of New York Authority, the Tri-State Planning Commission, and the Metropolitan Transportation Authority —whose functions overarch portions of three states. Finally, like the icing on the multilayered cake of political regulation and planning, federal regional agencies span the region.

Obviously the vast segmentation, overlapping of functions, and, indeed, competition for resources and territorial privilege among these more than 1,400 entities suggests the difficulty of securing the goal of rational planning in the NYMR. In some spheres of sensitive public interest such as the design of social services, housing, and educational programs, the situation borders on chaos.

Despite the fragmentation of governance, the well-integrated functioning of the American economic system as it affects the metropolitan land market has impressed a rough order on the region. The high access inner core predictably manifests an array of variegated and complex interrelated activities which are sensitive to communications in the metropolitan market—the commodity and stock markets; the fashion industry; the publishing industry; the media and advertising; a highly specialized medical care industry; retailing of high value commodities and specialty goods; and the numerous ancillary financial, legal, and consultative services upon which these industries depend. Vast residential areas, equally diversified, ring this core, from high density and high-rise luxury neighborhoods, to high density neighborhoods of poverty and disintegration, to low density communities of wealthy estates matched by low density poverty areas in desolate suburban pockets of despair. As residences have been developed farther out in the suburbs. economic activity has suburbanized as well. An outer zone of transportation, industry, and

warehousing has developed on the flatlands of New Jersey, on Long Island, and along the Connecticut shore.

But again, the rough order imposed by the economic system cuts across the patchwork of jurisdictions which are charged with controlling, planning, and managing the region for the benefit of the citizenry. In the jurisdictions most desperate for public services, the tax yield per capita is often low despite enormous local tax effort. An older municipality housing poor blue collar workers simply lacks the resource base of an affluent suburb like Princeton, New Jersey, where there is a concentration of wealth.

In a sense, the core and the peripheral industrial ring act in tandem as wealth-producing and wealth-distributing regions. The proceeds from this wealth are zones unequally divided among workers, management, and professional elites. Small trickles of income are carried by working class breadwinners to numerous lower middle class and poor neighborhoods close in around the core. More substantial dollar flows course to centers of affluence in the portfolios of the income elite. Since the major political decision-making boundary for many crucial service functions—like education, police, and welfare—is not drawn around the entire region, many small municipalities of poor people must make their decisions separated in economic benefit from the affluent municipalities of the rich. Income inequality is thus rigidified into inequality of municipal service consumption by the political fragmentation of the region, in contrast to its economic integration on the producing and distributing side. Now that state and federal controls are slowly smoothing out some services like education, planning efforts may gradually move the system toward greater equity in government services.

The fragmentation of the region raises control problems resembling what Paul Samuelson has suggested can lead to "the fallacy of composition." A person watching a soccer game and wanting a better view may stand on his seat. This strategy is a good one only if no one else follows it. What is good for an individual may not be good for the group. There are many public programs, development opportunities, and policies which to a community seem highly desirable. Yet if each community adopts such a program, disaster may ensue for the region. It seems splendid for a community to foster the development of an industrial park, which will bring in tax ratables, while at the same time enacting ordinances aimed at excluding school age population, perhaps by fostering the construction of two bedroom garden apartments and homes for the elderly and by expanding the lot requirements for private houses. Let the workers with families in the industrial park settle elsewhere—along with the educational burden of their children.

Of course, the neighboring communities adopt the same strategy. A housing crisis results for workers with families, employment problems develop for the firms, and a crushing commuting burden is imposed on the region as workers find themselves living far from their jobs.

Again, perhaps an upstream community on the Raritan or Hudson rivers decides to mini-

mize costs on waste treatment by pouring sewage into the water course: after all there is plenty of dissolved oxygen in the river to dissipate its waste load. Yet if all communities make the same decision, downstream reaches of these rivers run septic in the summer months, and portions of the New York–New Jersey estuarial system become dead seas, like the notorious Arthur Kill between Staten Island and New Jersey. Our society in general, and the NYMR in particular, has yet to learn how to cope with this class of problem.

With these preparatory comments about process, form, and control in mind, we now turn to the urban geography of specific sectors of the NYMR chosen to be representative of the more crucial aspects of these issues.

Commercial and Industrial Activities

There are four categories of goods and services production within the NYMR—manufacturing produces goods; retailing and wholesaling exchange goods at intermediate or final points of consumption; transportation and communication move goods and information from node to node within the system; and energy production and distribution drive the entire process.

MANUFACTURING INDUSTRY

The location of manufacturing industry within the NYMR changes constantly. At the turn of the century much of it would have been found at the cores of the cities of the region—New York, Newark, Paterson, Bridgeport, for example. Today, a centrifugal movement is well under way from the impetus of strong outward or centrifugal forces. The inward-directed, centripetal forces are by no means negligible, however, and we shall see through some industry examples how a variety of industrial activities are "centrifuged" outward, or remain at the core according to their intrinsic characteristics of land and labor requirements, marketing and financing attributes, and technological change, always coupled with the operation of chance and externalities.

Petrochemicals

The enormous market of the NYMR, coupled with its excellent seaport access to world sources of petroleum, virtually assured that a major petrochemical industry would arise to serve it. The labor requirements of this kind of industry are less pressing than those of more labor-intensive industries like garment manufacturing, and so, while access to residential areas attractive to skilled personnel is important, the number of journeys to work generated are insufficient to require a plant to relocate near the terminus of a major urban mass transportation system.

At the same time, the technology of the industry requires large, inexpensive allotments of land to such facilities as storage tank farms, cracking towers, processing complexes, and all of the space-consuming plumbing supporting the petrochemical industry. Access to rail, waterborne, truck, and pipeline modes of transportation are of great importance in combining the enormous tons of input materials and in marketing the final product.

In the more central and heavily urbanized areas of the region, not only are real estate values prohibitively high for the development of this kind of enterprise, but the parcels of land are very small. Even if an industry were willing and able to purchase a central tract for a plant, the negotiation for parcel acquisition in the tract can be extrordinarily difficult and expensive. In the end, a small number of hold out owners can imperil an entire scheme.

The preponderance of these factors argues for a peripheral rather than a central location for the petrochemical industry. Certain other industries which are oriented to a highly sensitive and changeable market (the New York Stock Exchange and the fashion industry come to mind) need speedy communication between customer, buyer, broker, producer, and financier on a day-to-day basis. Sometimes moment-to-moment information can be so crucial to survival that access to the center of the metropolitan switchboard overrides every consideration.

In the case of petroleum products, there are few differences among brands of gasoline, oil, and other petroleum and chemical products. There is thus little impetus for the firm to be located in the high cost metropolitan center. Indeed, since the differences among many of these products are largely imaginary, and fashions and fads in their consumption are produced not by manufacturing variations but by the imagination of advertising agencies, we do find a major concentration of advertising agencies in a high communications center on Madison Avenue in Midtown Manhattan.

In petrochemical manufacture, facilities cluster in massive complexes because the outputs of one set of plants are the inputs for others. Chemicals produced at basic refining complexes form the raw materials for other plants which produce paints, plastic, solvents, and other synthetic materials. Thus, the preponderance of locational influences tend to make the industry assume a perimeter rather than a core location, while technological considerations produce clustering. The industry is not spread out on the urban perimeter.

In the New Jersey coastal plain area to the south of Port Newark-Port Elizabeth, along the Arthur Kill which separates Staten Island from the mainland, we find all of the conditions discussed here fulfilled. Adjacent to the giant petrochemical installations of Exxon, Texaco, Hess, Reichold Chemical, and many others may be found the main line of the Jersey Central and the Penn Central, the New Jersey Turnpike, the natural gas pipeline from Texas nicknamed "the Big Inch," the two giant container ports, Newark Airport providing convenient air freight and management access, and tanker berths all along the Arthur Kill. Some of the companies are interconnected with each other by pipes, so that direct delivery of a product manufactured by one plant and required by another is accomplished with a minimum of transportation cost and with direct billing through an automatic metering system.

But metropolitan expansion has engulfed this complex of petrochemical plumbing. Once at the fringe of the urbanized core, urbaniza-

tion has leapfrogged over this industrial area deep into New Jersey, hemming it in so that large tracts of open land for expansion are no longer easily acquired. Other plants have become obsolete and may be phased out, as in the case of Hess. The development of supertankers and the competitive economics which attend their use have made the Arthur Kill obsolete as a tanker port, for not only is the thirty-five foot deep channel inadequate for the largest modern vessels, but also the turning radii from New York Bay into the Kill van Kull (north of Staten Island) and thence into the Arthur Kill are far too sharp to accommodate them.

The external diseconomies of the petroleum complex to the region have been great. The industries of the NYMR contribute to the largest air and water pollution problem in the nation. Waste discharges, oil spills, and tanker traffic have played a part in rendering the waters of the Arthur Kill and part of the Kill van Kull septic for part of the year. These waters are so polluted that they could not even be purified by massive distillation. The boiling points of some of the complex chemical pollutants are the same as that of water.

One hundred years ago these waters were the pride of a flourishing oyster and shellfish industry. Today there are reaches which are so contaminated that even sewage bacteria cannot survive in them. The effects of this kind of pollution of the marine ecology of an important estuarial and offshore environment are poorly understood, but, coupled with garbage scow dumping and the unsatisfactory treatment of sewage waste effluent introduced in these waters, an extensive "dead sea" has developed in the New Jersey-New York Bight between the Raritan and Hudson rivers. Since seashore recreation is a major industry on the New Jersey Atlantic shore the inhabitants there are understandably skeptical about the development of a deep-water port and offshore oil drilling in their vicinity, with its attendant dangers of spillage and pollution.

Will the petrochemical industry on which the NYMR market depends find the means to grow and modernize in the midst of a public increasingly sensitive to issues involving environmental degradation? What are the alternatives? Relocation of the industry within the crowded region with its incredible fixed investment in plant seems impossible. Limitation of its growth could possibly put a brake on regional growth in industries which depend on cheap petroleum products. These industries are key elements for regional employment patterns. Yet, the price to be paid by the region for continued growth to meet demand might very well be ecologically disastrous for the estuarial environment and the air quality over many urbanized portions of the region. There does not really exist a planning mechanism by which these dilemmas may be rigorously attacked.

The Garment Industry

The garment district of Manhattan, located on the west side of the island in the numerous industrial lofts extending through streets north of 34th Street and focused on Seventh Avenue, has become a part of American folklore. It represents an industry which is strongly agglomerated like petrochemicals, but centrally rather than peripherally located.

The casual visitor strolling around the district during the peak period of its operation may well wonder how any business can possibly survive in the midst of the incredible traffic congestion and human clamor which fills the streets during working hours. The visible negative externalities would seem to choke and stifle any enterprise located here. How does it survive?

The core of the industry is the manufacture of women's and misses' ready to wear garments. Traditionally, this industry has been highly sensitive to the dictates of fashion and intensive in its use of skilled labor, with numerous small and sometimes ephemeral firms and unusual seasonal financing and capital requirements, and is highly seasonal in its operation.

These observations may be summed up by noting that in regard to the requirements of loft space, labor capital, marketing, and finance, it is an extraordinarily nonstandardized industry. Whereas the differences between one brand of gasoline and another may be insignificant, the differences between a "hot number" and a dud in the garment trade spells the difference between success and failure.

These considerations have led to the development of a remarkable and subtle supporting infrastructure of positive externalities in the district. The area is centrally accessible to labor residing all over the region by means of the highly developed West Side subway facilities of Manhattan, the Port Authority bus terminal at

42nd Street which connects with most of the northern New Jersey suburbs, and the Pennsylvania Railroad Station which immediately adjoins the district. These facilities serve a population of more than ten million people. In addition, the needle trades unions maintain hiring facilities in the district.

An extensive market in loft space also exists in the district, with rental arrangements tailored to the highly variable nature of the industry. Closely related to this is a highly developed capital goods market (sewing machines, cutting equipment, and so forth) enabling failing firms to turn over assets quickly to the benefit of the newly established firm. In a similar fashion certain banks and financial institutions such as the Chemical Bank of New York have developed a specialization in the unusual short term types of financing required by garment district firms.

Certain processing firms provide manufacturing services in everything from embroidering to button making. This enables a dress firm to avoid the expense of establishing its own embroidery department for a special style which may have only a short fashion run.

The successful manufacturer not only possesses a top designing staff, but also has a finger on the pulse of the very best deal available in securing his loft space, labor, capital, financing, and subcontracting. A good cutter in his labor force can so arrange the cutting of the basic cloth to the required pattern that wastage is minimized in production. Access to good quality used equipment and the saving of a point or two of interest in financing may mean survival.

There is a highly interconnected garment manufacturing subculture which is extremely interdependent. The central persons in the communications network of this subculture have the edge on being successful in an extraordinarily competitive field.

Our emphasis on the external economies available to the production end of the business should not obscure similar conditions which prevail on the sales end of the business. The chief customers of the garment center manufacturing firms are major department stores throughout not only the NYMR, but also the country. The agglomeration of so many of these firms into the Seventh Avenue district has led to the development of a highly organized fashion market. Buyers from all over the country flock to the district for the purpose of securing new seasonal fashion lines for the stores which they represent. The manufacturing firms are poised for this event by having the best of their newly designed fashion apparel available for showings. Contingency plans have been made to take on the necessary additional equipment, labor, financing, material, and ancillary services should a big order ensue.

The buyers' season results in spin-off demand for other business services in Midtown Manhattan, ranging from cinema and legitimate theater entertainment, night clubs, and restaurant and hotel services, to illicit services in the immediate vicinity of Seventh Avenue.

Access to this market, and to the buyers' annual visits, is the sine qua non of the successful garment entrepreneur. The year's profits depend on the comparative advantage of the firm's line in this brief span of time.

Recently, some garment manufacturers have become sufficiently large and diversified that they have enough business volume to generate their own specialized ancillary departments, year round labor force, and long term capital and financial arrangements. Such large scale firms can afford to separate themselves from the external economies of production in the garment district and move elsewhere—to the South, for example, where labor and materials may be cheaper. Even these firms, however, tend to retain showroom space where some of their designers may remain in close contact with fashion trends.

Nevertheless, there has been erosion in New York's garment district. Lines of garments such as uniforms and undergarments which are made in long runs and are less sensitive to fashion have long since begun to move away from Seventh Avenue to lower cost locations in the hinterlands. The flag industry—a finished textile industry, although not a garment industry— moved all the way to Puerto Rico.

Finally, major fashion markets have arisen in the South and West following changes in consumer preference for clothing—casual over formal, western style over eastern, and the vogue for jeans and levis. These shifts have undercut Seventh Avenue's prosperity, relative importance, and employment, causing great concern in the New York City government.

All of these factors add up to a loss of manufacturing jobs in Manhattan. The fashion-sensitive functions of the portion of the indus-

try remaining in the NYMR will probably continue to be aggregated and centrally located, at least in the short run, but the industry as a whole is gravely weakened.

THE FINANCIAL INDUSTRY

The Manhattan yellow pages list four full four column pages of stock and bond brokers. One estimates well above 1,000 listings, of which only a handful are outside of the triangular district of lower Manhattan known as Wall Street. In the securities industry and its financial auxiliaries, *information* is the quintessential commodity about which all else revolves. In the precise concretization of the switchboard metaphor of Deutsch, the stock exchange established itself as closely as possible to the seaport message source, with its roots going back informally to 1792, and formally to 1817. Ship lookouts with telescopes on the roofs of buildings, ship-to-office couriers, fire signalmen on Staten Island, and privilege riders in pilot boats all played a part in the nineteenth century marketing of information. Today, the Wall Street district is a maze of information exchange mechanisms.

A system of swift bonded couriers are used for the transfer of special financial paper. They know the shortest point-to-point routings in the area, using basement tunnels and sequestered alleyways in some cases. They are assisted by firms providing armed guards and armored trucks for important financial shipments. Five such firms operate in and near the financial district, including one which specializes in air courier service. The usual media—telephone, telegraph, stock ticker—are supplemented by elaborate computer-data-processing connections. One major bank in the district built a second multifloor building only a few blocks away on some of the highest priced real estate on earth to house its mammoth data-processing functions.

Despite a recent major upgrading of the data-processing system of the New York Stock Exchange, it has outgrown its classic 1903 building at Broad and Wall streets and plans have been made to move it to a landfill site at the Fulton Fish Market location on the East River near Wall Street.

As with brokerage houses, so with banks. Most of the major commercial banks in the world have a substantial commitment in office space in the Wall Street district. From "Algemene Bank Nederland, N.V." to "Wells Fargo Bank International Corp.," there are well over one hundred bank headquarters in the Wall Street area, representing American giants like Chase Manhattan, First National City, and Marine Midland as well as American headquarters for numerous foreign banking firms.

Among the institutional fixtures of the district are the New York Customs House; Federal Reserve Bank of New York; Federal Deposit Insurance Corporation; Securities and Exchange Commission; Federal Home Loan Mortgage Corporation; the Cocoa, Coffee, Sugar, Commodity, Cotton, Wool, and Produce Exchanges, the New York Clearing House; and the World Trade Center. This complex of finance, brokerage, exchange, insurance, and ancillary services is unparalleled in the western hemisphere and has the world as its region.

As a measure of the vigor which still attaches to Wall Street, it may be pointed out that in the boom years of 1925-1933, 138 buildings with an aggregate floor area of 30.4 million square feet were built in all of Manhattan including Wall Street. In the years 1967-1972 alone, for the downtown office area only, seventeen buildings with an aggregate footage of 214 million were built or nearing completion, including the ten million square foot World Trade Center. Thus, seventeen buildings in the late 1960s and early 1970s provide two-thirds the square footage, in the financial district alone, that the entire "Roaring Twenties" provided for all of Manhattan.

Since 1972, however, stagnation has increasingly affected the development of even this traditional Manhattan activity. Suburbanization and regional decentralization is occurring in the securities industry.

ADVERTISING

What Wall Street is to finance, the East midtown area (from the Forties north and centered on Madison Avenue) is to advertising. Well over 1,000 advertising agencies and counselors are listed, the greatest concentration of which are found in and near the Madison Avenue district. Surrounding and permeating this district is the midtown Manhattan concentration of banking and financial institutions. Two of the great Wall Street banks (Manufacturers Hanover, First National City) have established a "dual head-

quarters" structure, dividing midtown and downtown operations. The banking facilities available in midtown are second only to the Wall Street district.

One of the reasons for the dual center is the migration and concentration of headquarters functions of major American corporations into the midtown area. By 1970, about 120 of the 500 largest industrial concerns in the nation (almost 25 percent) and about forty of the 250 largest nonindustrial concerns (16 percent) had established their headquarters in New York. Virtually all of the others maintain major regional offices there. Banks are drawn to the center of such corporate concentration.

In addition, to the west of Madison Avenue lies Rockefeller Center and the focus of entertainment and radio and TV activities—especially theater and television. To the east lies the United Nations district, abounding with national trade missions and consulates with public relations problems. Downtown, along Park Avenue South, lies a district rich in technical specialists in all aspects of the design, graphics, and photographic trades.

Madison Avenue enjoys the distinction of being within a pleasant walk of more potential corporate customers than, perhaps, anywhere else in the Western Hemisphere. Once their media needs are established, the theatrical district and the graphic arts firms supply the personnel and technical help. Television and other media are immediately at hand to diffuse the product; and—if the client is recalcitrant—some of the best restaurants, shops, and theater in the world lie within a few blocks to soften moods.

The result of Manhattan's attractiveness for such functions as corporate headquarters, advertising, finance, and related activities may be gauged by the fact that, since 1947, some 212 major buildings which aggregate to more than 94,910,000 square feet of office space have been built there. Most of this construction has spread out from the UN nucleus on 42nd Street and the East River. The other major growth center has been Wall Street.

While the spurt of development which has followed the demolition and subsequent replacement of a run-down warehouse and factory district by the beautiful architecture and carefully landscaped center of a world organization is a textbook case of the spillover effect of an urban amenity upon neighboring space, there was strong evidence by the mid-1970s that the offices were overbuilt. A tendency for major firms to move headquarters functions to the suburbs of the NYMR is now viewed with concern by the city's administration. If central office functions suburbanize—like manufacturing, wholesaling, retailing, and shipping—the essence of Manhattan's viability as an economic entity will have been undermined.

PUBLISHING AND PRINTING

More than 600 book publishers or branch offices of publishers are listed in Manhattan. A few are giants—McGraw-Hill, John Wiley, Charles Scribner, Simon and Schuster, and Random House, for example. Many more are tiny specialized firms catering to a limited market. Most are located in midtown Manhattan; the largest close to 42nd Street on the East Side near the UN, the smaller ones stretching to the south and north.

Aside from the obvious advantages of Midtown Manhattan for book publishing—access to publicity and the media, access to an enormous pool of skilled and professional workers by means of the metropolitan mass transit systems which converge at midtown, and access to the worldwide network of financial institutions which have long experience in the needs of activities like publishing—there are special local advantages external to the firm which favor Manhattan.

The presence of the New York intellectual community is extremely important from the standpoint of book criticism, manuscript evaluation, and the generation of publishable manuscripts themselves. Located at 42nd Street and Fifth Avenue is a great literary resource, the New York Public Library. Moreover, in the side streets of East midtown numerous small specialized libraries provide collections unduplicated elsewhere—the Morgan Library, the Mercantile Library Association, the Library of the Regional Plan Association, and libraries which belong to universities or to professional organizations of architects, engineers, and unions, not to mention the UN.

In a manner analogous to the garment center, there has been a tendency for activities related to manufacturing—like book printing and warehousing—to move out of the intellectual, media, and entertainment center of New York, but few enterprises have followed the lead of Prentice-Hall or Pergamon Press in establishing themselves in the suburbs. More typical is Oxford University Press, which maintains editorial and executive offices on Madison Avenue, while keeping its customer service functions in a suburban location in Fair Lawn, New Jersey. But even the New Jersey office has a direct tie New York City telephone number.

Book publishing remains concentrated in New York State (Table 1). A slight fall-off in percentage contribution in all of the states in the list was matched by an increase in Massachusetts. Since New York State really emphasizes the NYMR, and Massachusetts means largely the Boston Metropolitan Region, it seems that the areas richest in support services needed by publishers are also strongest in book publishing. By contrast, whereas the New York SMSA had 21 percent of

Table 1. Book Publishing by Leading States

| | Establishments | | Number Employed | | | |
| | | | 1954 | | 1967 | |
	1954	1967	(1,000s)	Percent	(1,000s)	Percent
U.S. Total	814	1022	34.7	100	51.8	100
New York State	333	349	15.9	46	21.4	41
Illinois	88	112	5.9	17	8.0	15
Wisconsin	15	19	2.1	6	–	–
Pennsylvania	39	47	1.7	5	1.8	3
Minnesota	23	19	1.5	4	2.4	5
Massachusetts	39	57	1.4	4	5.5	11

Source: W. Eric Gustafson "Printing and Publishing," in Max Hall, ed., *Made in New York*, ch. 2 (Cambridge, Mass.: Harvard University Press, 1959); and U.S. Census.

United States book production workers in 1954 (as against publishing,) by 1967 it had dropped to 15 percent.

The printing establishments in the city (in contrast to publishing) cluster in areas in which the demand for their services is substantial. At City Hall Plaza, where city and state bureaucracies and court functions are to be found, there is a massive assortment of law offices, bail bondsmen, and printers serving the city's legal trade. Other printing shops are found along the edges of midtown, in the upper floors of office and loft buildings, holding on to the coattails of the advertising and media worlds. All of these functions respond more to centripetal than to centrifugal forces, while petrochemicals and certain lines of retail and wholesale merchandising have been "centrifuged"outward.

A key is the role played by nearby supportive services available to the firm. These are called "external economies." Publishing depends on such external economies as are found in midtown Manhattan. Printing shops collectively form one of these external economies and, in turn, depend on publishing houses for their own trade. They are two terms in a symbiotic equation.

RETAILING AND WHOLESALING

The specialized activities that have as their aim the distribution of goods and services to the general population must strike a careful balance between central and perimeter location. Pulling wholesaling to the center, for example, is access by way of the shortest route to the largest market. Major components of this market are restaurants, caterers, and food retailing establishments which have traditionally had a core city location. Other things being equal, the optimum location for wholesaling activities would lie at the transportation nodes closest to the center of metropolitan population—that is, Manhattan Island. And, indeed, for many more than a hundred years, the various wholesaling districts for produce, butter and eggs, fish and meats, to name a few responded to this rule and could be found in stable locations in Manhattan. They could thus distribute to both core and outer rim markets by efficient transportation connections.

But today, "other things are not equal," and some wholesaling functions are being drawn outward from the core. The first and possibly the most important factor is demographic. Inner regions of the city like Manhattan and Brooklyn lose their residential popularity as business uses multiply and the population that remains is diminishing in density. Instead of a densely occupied central city tapering off to more rarified suburbs, it is convenient to imagine a "doughnut" of population with a small but growing central "hole" occupied largely by commercial uses, surrounded by suburbs of thinner densities.

Pulled out to doughnut locations have been restaurant, catering, and retailing establishments that serve the suburbs. As time goes on, the hole is growing and the doughnut increasing in overall diameter. The time has come when certain types of wholesaling—of foods and perishable items in particular—are more effectively done from a "doughnut" location (in terms of efficient access to retailers) than a "hole" location.

This tendency has been reinforced by the development of circumferential regional transportation routes and by the clogging up of central radial routes by traffic overloads. The availability of land for more spacious perimeter terminal facilities also contrasts with the cramped facilities and limited expansion possibilities at the city center.

Since New York City is located on a set of islands, rail connection with all of New York except the Bronx is largely accomplished by carfloat, railferry, and a few intermittently opening bridges. The logic of these conditions of site difficulty, when coupled with the demographic growth imperative of the city, has drawn wholesaling and warehousing activity into more peripheral locations. The food and produce markets of lower Manhattan are relocating. Wholesaling has moved, in these cases, to the giant new Hunt's Point terminal in the Bronx—a location which maximizes truck access to inner and outer ring population and retailing centers of the region by means of circumferential routes, while retaining the delivery capability to retailers at the core by radial ones.

To the west, in the New Jersey meadowlands, especially in the region roughly extending between Newark and Hackensack, an immense amount of light manufacturing, warehousing, and terminal activity has sprung up, partly on landfill. This location, on its inner flank, adjoins the New Jersey Turnpike, major circumferential highways, the Central of New Jersey and Penn Central classification yards, the ports of Newark and Elizabeth, and the Newark Airport. On its outer flank is found the major concentration of residential suburbs in northern New Jersey.

If wholesale activity is responding to the impulse for centrifugal movement, retailing is even more strongly suburbanizing. Major outlying shopping centers have sprung up in a ring throughout the demographic "doughnut" where major radial and circumferential access routes cross. In this sense, New York does not differ from other metropolitan regions where economic activity is suburbanizing.

In New York, however, the central business district retains great vitality. While residential population no longer exists in such great abundance in Manhattan, the diurnal working population is enormous. Furthermore, the range and diversification of goods which may be purchased in just a few square blocks of midtown Manhattan is perhaps unparalleled on the globe. One major bank (the Drydock Savings Bank) has used this theme in advertising in order to persuade its customers to "bank in Drydock Country, where everything is."

Two kinds of retailing continue to show great vigor in Manhattan. The first is the specialty good or service, for which Manhattan is the center of a regional or even worldwide network of buyers. Art galleries, tapestries, antiques, fine furniture, opera, theater, concerts, and jewelry are but a few. The *range* or distance which customers will travel in person or through agents to make a purchase is large, and the *threshold* or gross dollar volume of business which the firm must do in order to break even is large. These firms find it worthwhile to bear the large operating costs of prestigious Manhattan locations such as Fifth Avenue, Madison Avenue, or, in the case of entertainment enterprises, Broadway or Lincoln Center.

The second type of retailing which is vigorous in Manhattan is that which serves either the diurnal working population (novelty, notions, drug, cosmetic, restaurant, and haberdashery establishments, for instance) or the places where they work. Office furniture and equipment, commercial linen services, and window washing firms provide one type of example. Specialized music-retailing firms which serve the opera and concert world; art appraisal firms; and the firms of the diamond

center which buy and sell, cut, and set stones are other examples of firms which have other basic businesses as their customers.

The medical industry, which retails health services extensively in the region, is a useful example. A number of major medical facilities of worldwide repute catering to highly specialized needs and health problems are concentrated along the East River, both north and south of the midtown business district. Auxiliary activities ranging from laboratories and medical supply firms to major research institutes provide services directly to this complex of health care facilities. By virtue of the enormous *range* (people come from the antipodes to avail themselves of the services) and the high *threshold* (occasioned by the cost of equipment, plant, and medical labor), this service-retailing industry occupies a central Manhattan location.

In contrast, other kinds of medical retailing (the general practitioner and the small group) have tended to follow population and purchasing power to the suburbs. And so, as in the case of merchandise retailing, where convenience goods and standard lines of widely purchased durable goods have moved to suburban shopping centers while highly specialized retailing functions remain in the city, major medical functions remain in the city and more common branches of practice have moved to the suburbs. Thus, in the suburbs, one can buy reproductions of paintings suitable for framing (but not an original Braque), or standard kinds of medical service (but not treatment for a rare and complex ailment).

Such movement and relocation tends to leave on the inside rim of the doughnut an area of poor tenement neighborhoods badly served both by retailers in the process of closing and moving out and, especially, by medical practitioners who are retiring or moving away with no replacements in sight.

The overall pattern set forth here is complicated by topography and the configuration of waterways, which, in turn, are reflected in the pattern of transportation routes, and by the occurrence of state, city, and municipal boundaries that separate regions of differing sales, income, and business tax regulations. Occasionally retailing activity is thinner on the more highly sales-taxed New York City side than on the Nassau County side, for example, of the boundary of western Queens. The major new shopping centers on Long Island are all in Nassau County rather than Queens. Gasoline stations often thin out sharply as one drives north from New Jersey into New York state.

But withal, the density of purchasing power in the outer band of the expanding population "doughnut" coupled with the growing central commercial "hole" in which jobs are intensively concentrated is driving a process of functional separation and redistribution of both wholesaling and retailing activity in the region.

TRANSPORTATION

That transportation feature in the New York metropolitan region that sets it off from most other metropolitan regions is its general cargo container port. Its counterpart is found in the Rhine Delta container port area, since New York's container port and that of the Rhine Delta are really simply two stations on an intercontinental conveyor belt.

The port of New York has undergone a series of transformations during its 300 years, with the container ports as the logical latest stage. The cramped finger piers and canals built along the East River side of Manhattan south of Wall Street by the Dutch gave way to the expansion of the East River and, later, the Hudson River waterfronts. Already bustling by the midnineteenth century, port facilities spilled across the East River to Brooklyn and beyond the Hudson River to Hoboken.

Ever pressed by the squeeze of congestion and costs of delay on the landward side combined with development pressures raising Manhattan real estate values, the Manhattan seaport was already doomed by World War I. Brooklyn had assumed the dominant shipping role by then. But, inexorably, the technological and managerial revolution which has dominated general cargo handling since World War II eventually led to the obsolescence of the great expanse of Brooklyn dock area and the concomitant development of Port Newark–Port Elizabeth as the center of life in the port of New York and New Jersey. It is now appropriate to recognize the addition of the term "New Jersey" to the title of that entity.

To illustrate today's port operations let us consider what happens when a freight shipment is consigned at an inland location like Schenectady, New York, for delivery at, say, Dusseldorf in West Germany (Figure 7).

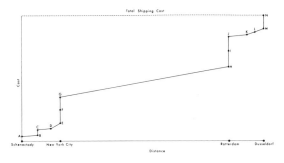

Figure 7. Shipping Costs before Containerization.

- The first increment to the shipping cost (A) represents initial loading costs on a truck or railroad car.
- The rise in cost between A and B represents shipping costs into the New York City area.
- The vertical line between B and C represents the cost of a traffic jam, dead cost of driver salary, and stationary vehicle.
- Shipment resumes between C and D.
- Costs rise to E as shipment slows getting to the dock.
- Unloading costs at the dockside, plus pilferage and insurance, or both, bring charges to F.
- Slowness of loading means a longer turnaround time in port. Part of cost of maintaining the vessel in port is borne by the shipper, raising charges to G.
- Costs of shipment to Rotterdam bring the aggregate cost to H.
- Unloading, pilferage, and insurance in Rotterdam raise costs to I.
- A portion of the vessel turnaround costs related to slow unloading by stevedore gangs jacks the shipping cost to J.
- Movement inland by truck adds cost between J and K.
- Increased costs of congestion between K and L upon nearing the Rhur district.
- Dusseldorf destination is reached at M.
- Final unloading costs raise the total shipping bill to N.

This sequence of events is a simplified version of the traditional shipping process. At Port Newark–Port Elizabeth, however, landward and waterward means of transportation are drawn together in an unprecedented fashion. Thirty-six deepwater berths are available along two thirty-five foot deep channels constructed in filled land along the western shore of Newark Bay. The landward extension of the facilities covers more than 1,400 acres and provides for wide aprons, ample warehousing space, and more than four million square feet of paved upland area. Already, by 1973, this port was handling more than 20 percent of the general cargo of the metropolitan region—the largest general cargo handling port in the nation.

Gantry cranes stand ready at the dockside to load trailer truck boxes, railroad car boxes, lighters, or standardized containers (depending on the nature of the vessel and the company concerned) on shipboard in a matter of minutes per container, cutting port turnaround time to a minimum. Many vessels can now arrive in port, unload, reload, and sail the next day. Thus, vessels with a capacity of more than 1,000 trailer truck boxes can be almost continuously in use.

Furthermore, pilferage is inhibited because the shipper seals his cargo into a container which is not opened again until it reaches its ultimate destination. Thus, insurance costs drop. In 1973, a record year, only one container load was stolen.

Immediately adjacent to Port Newark–Port Elizabeth are the New Jersey Turnpike, Newark Airport, and the main lines of four major railroads, including the Jersey Central and Penn Central lines. All have connections with complexes of wharfside cargo distribution buildings. The Penn Central International Container Terminal at Port Newark is capable of handling trainloads of up to sixty cars. Under these circumstances, the facilities are within overnight, second morning or third morning delivery to over one hundred million people in the United States (Figure 8).

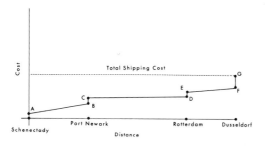

Figure 8. Shipping Costs after Containerization.

With traffic delays, turnaround delays, and pilferage controlled, and with fast motorship transportation provided, the total cost is cut greatly. Automated terminals have been developed in this great port complex to handle frozen goods such as meat, bananas, wine (by pipeline from tank ships), lumber, and general cargo.

In addition, there are two on site commercial bank branches serving Port Newark–Port Elizabeth. In a manner comparable to the technology which has smoothed the seams in goods transportation between the water mode and the land modes, information transmission systems have been developed that send invoices, manifests, and commercial paper parallel to the goods shipment so that dockside and customer clearances may be expedited.

The location of the container ports at Newark Bay is part and parcel of a pattern of centripetal movement in shipping facilities which has gone on in the port of New York for a long time. For more than 400 years urbanization has pushed seaport acitivites progressively further from the downtown city center. By the 1850s the seaport had migrated north along Manhattan's East River shore nearby to the newly created landfill area beyond the present location of the Williamsburg Bridge. A small but tightly knit colony of Norwegians engaged in the maritime trade worked near the docks and lived in a portion of the lower East Side.

By 1870, port activity was pushed to Brooklyn across the river near Furman Street. From 1870–1910 the Norwegians, following their livelihood, resided in adjoining areas of Brooklyn, today a hopelessly obsolescent site despite Port Authority efforts to modernize the area. At a cost of $94 million, a two mile long system of twelve modern steel and concrete piers with twenty-seven berths and a capacity of 3.5 million tons of cargo per year have been installed. At its heyday, 4,300 jobs were provided here, but, despite all efforts, landward connections are unsatisfactory, cramped by the cliff of Brooklyn Heights. The railroad line located here is only two miles long and offers no landward connection to any mainline. Remembering that Brooklyn is part of an island, like most of New York City, rail connections are few (Figure 9).

In other cities, rail junctions bring ocean freight inland to a spider web of radial and circumferential railroad lines by which goods may

Figure 9. Brooklyn Waterfront Cramped between the East River and the Foot of Montague Street. Note tugboat in float bridge slip at left.

be switched inland and laterally to a variety of sidings and yards. Chicago is usually taken as typical. The port of New York–New Jersey lacks the complete development of circumferential belt lines, so carfloats, lighters, and barges perform this circumferential transfer function. The vast marshaling yards on the New Jersey mainland and the yards at Sunnyside–Long Island City in Queens serve this ferrying operation by means of float bridges, such as the one which serves the Furman Street facility.

Overloaded even by the 1890s, the Brooklyn waterfront pushed to the still more decentralized location at the Bush Terminals. In the 1890s, as the North Brooklyn docks were feeling pressure, Irving Bush began to develop this terminal district based upon the concept of coordinating landward and seaward transportation with industrial processes through a site plan which brings railroad sidings from piers into the center of factory blocks. Located on the side of his father's oil business, it covers 200 acres, comprises eighteen piers with three

berths on each side, 150 six to twelve story building units, and its own railroad (the Bush Terminal Railroad), unconnected directly with any main line. At its peak, its industries employed 30,000 workers (Figure 10).

Today it is obsolescent as a port facility. Vertical loft buildings are unsatisfactory for many kinds of manufacturing. Inadequate landward transportation connections by road and rail are a handicap. Instead of a flow of materials to factory and goods to market over the integrated transportation arrangements, the toymaking, textile, garment, and novelty firms in the lofts today have little need for rail and ship transportation. Conversely, the palletized and containerized ship operations nearby serve the general urban region rather than chiefly the Bush Terminals.

When port expansion was dictated by the shipping needs of World War I, a less central location was again developed immediately to the south of the Bush terminals. In 1917, in response to the shipping pressure in World War I,

(A)

(B)

Figure 10. **(A)** Bush Terminal Buildings, Brooklyn. To the left is the waterfront and a dockside railroad. To the right, surface roads connect with Brooklyn. Rail sidings penetrate the interior bays of the buildings. **(B)** Bush Terminal Buildings, Brooklyn. Interior bay showing railroad sidings.

Irving Bush was made chairman of the War Board of New York. The Brooklyn Army Base was built, with 3.8 million square feet of storage space and sidings for 450 railroad cars. It is connected by land with the marshaling yards at the Penn Central in Queens. At its peak, it has had 60,000 jobs. In World War II, half of the troops and one-third of the supplies sent overseas from the United States went through this terminal.

In adjoining Sunset Park and Bay Ridge, the Norwegian colony which we remarked in Brooklyn by 1879 was present by 1910, corresponding to shifts in maritime trades activity. Vestiges of this colony can still be seen, suggesting how the suburbanizing of the maritime trades and its working force have gone hand in hand.

The latest stage in the process of port decentralization is Port Newark–Port Elizabeth, close to railroad, thruway, and airport. On the northern side of the Newark Channel is the Auto Port where specialized carriers of European and Japanese cars unload. Container ship facilities are located on the south side. Also located in this zone is a palletized lumber port and an automated wine terminal. An overhead pipeline brings wine from tanker ships to a bottling and distribution facility (Figure 11).

On the north side of the Elizabeth Channel is the scrap steel port, facing the container ports on the south side. The massive cranes which serve the port cost more than $1 million each and roll along 5,000 feet of bulkhead by railroad track. These cranes can accommodate twenty, twenty-four, thirty-five, and forty foot containers. They illustrate how heavily capitalized the modern port is. Large areas of land for storage terminals and truck marshaling, along with the intensive use of machinery, substitute for labor.

THE LANDSCAPE OF ENERGY

The functions of the metropolis which we have so far discussed in this study—manufacturing, retailing, wholesaling, and transportation—are driven by energy. Driving to New York City by way of the New Jersey Turnpike, one cannot help noticing the landscape of energy which develops north of Carteret. To the left are the gas and petroleum pipelines which serve the metropolis. To the right, beside the Arthur Kill separating New Jersey from Staten Island,

are oilport facilities, tank farms, and petrochemical complexes. At the northern end of the turnpike is a giant thermal electric plant of the Public Service Gas and Electric Company of New Jersey. This region is one of the giant engines that drives the metropolis. What is the significance of this scene? Five sources of energy—coal, oil, gas, hydraulic flow, and nuclear fission—drive a series of electric generation plants, which are linked together into a system affording electricity to the metropolitan power market. Additionally, some coal, oil, and gas pass directly to metropolitan consumers without going through the intervening step of electric conversion.

If the metropolitan power market exercised a steady, unchanging demand it would be possible, theoretically at least, to bring the entire flow system into such nice balance that the fuel imports, conversion rates, and power outputs would be exactly in equilibrium, with no need for system adjustments to varying supplies or demands. Such is not the case, however, and there exist great fluctuations in the demand for power in the metropolitan region on a regular diurnal, weekly, and seasonal basis. Additionally, there is an annual trend for power demands to increase.

The above implies that due to daily, weekly, seasonally, and annually fluctuating demands (and failures of supply as well), storage and back-up capacity must be available at all times. This is provided by coal yards, oil tanks, and gas tanks which maintain surplus capacity to fill sudden needs. The Consolidated Edison Company of New York has also proposed a special pump storage facility atop the highlands overlooking the Hudson River at Cornwall, north of the city. This facility would comprise a reservoir and a pumping and generating station. During periods of surplus power, water would be pumped up out of the Hudson River to the reservoir, while during periods of power shortage, the water would be released to fall back to the river, driving turbogenerators on the way, and thus reconverting the potential energy of the raised water into needed electrical energy.

Within the context of this discussion, one can envision energy in the form of coal from Appalachia; electricity from the hydroelectric stations on the Canadian frontier; oil and gas from the South and from overseas; fission fuel from Oak Ridge, Tennessee, destined for

(A)

(B)

Figure 11. Port Newark-Elizabeth: **(A)** Scrap steel port. Ship being loaded with electromagnet cranes. **(B)** Trailer-truck-sized container being loaded on a container ship by a gantry crane.

(C)

(D)

(C) Imported Japanese automobiles await shipment inland. **(D)** Palletized lumber bundles await shipment inland.

the Indian Point fission electric plant on the Hudson River, all converging by every conceivable means on the metropolis, and especially on northeastern New Jersey, to be transformed into the power needs of America's primate metropolitan area.

The effects of this metropolitan power landscape are great; refinery storage tank areas, coal yards, railway yards, pipelines, wharf facilities, transmission lines, generating plants, and relay stations are all part of it.

Residential Space

THE BASIC HOUSING STOCK

Most residents of the metropolitan region live in multiple dwellings. In 1970 in New York City, 2.2 million out of 2.9 million units were rental units. In the New York City portion of the region, this housing stock can be subdivided into the following categories:

- Pre-1867 multiple dwellings
- "Old Law tenements" built between 1867 and 1901
- "New Law tenements" built between 1901 and 1929
- Post-1929 structures
- Rented one or two family houses (Table 2)

Table 2. Renter-Occupied Housing Units by Structure Type, New York City, 1970

Structure Type	Units (1,000s)	Percent
Old Law	248	12
New Law	756	36
Post-1929	616	30
Others	169	8
Rented Houses	265	13
Total	2,024	100
Unaccounted for	143	–

Source: George Sternlieb and James W. Hughes, *Housing and People in New York City* (New York: The Housing and Development Administration of the City of New York, Department of Rent and Housing Maintenance, 1973).

The rented houses tend to be located in newer areas on the perimeter of the non-Manhattan boroughs. The bulk of the housing in Manhattan and the inner areas of Brooklyn, the Bronx, and Queens was built before 1929, and a substantial amount prior to 1901. This observation is reinforced when we consider that many residences in the "other" category consist of nineteenth century (or earlier) townhouses which have been subdivided, flats constructed prior to the Old Tenement Law of 1867, or vintage buildings originally constructed for nonresidential purposes. In Greenwich Village (Manhattan) and Brooklyn Heights (Brooklyn) there are numerous carriage houses located on eighteenth and nineteenth century mews which have been converted to residential use. In the cast iron building section—south of Houston Street in Manhattan; called the SoHo district locally—there are likewise numerous factory lofts dating from the 1870s which have been illegally converted to residential use. Table 3 presents a breakdown by borough.

More than half of Manhattan's 613,000 rented units were built before 1929. Brooklyn and the Bronx reveal comparable patterns. Only partly suburban Queens and Staten Island deviate from this pattern. This is not to say that age inexorably implies decrepitude. A small percentage of Old Law and New Law tenements command high rentals, while some post-1929 dwellings and rental houses eke out very small rentals. In any era there is shoddy as well as sound construction, and some early structures, by virtue of their careful construction, quality

Table 3.   Rental Housing in New York City, by Type, by Borough, 1970 (percent)

Structure Type	Bronx	Brooklyn	Manhattan	Queens	Staten Island
Old Law	4	12	25	1	1
New Law	59	36	30	22	4
Post-1929	29	24	30	45	33
Others	3	8	14	4	4
Rented Houses	6	19	1	28	57
Total	100	100	100	100	100
Units (1,000s)	406	622	613	354	28

Source: George Sternlieb and James W. Hughes, *Housing and People in New York City* (New York: The Housing and Development Administration of the City of New York, Department of Rent and Housing Maintenance, 1973).

materials, and neighborhood amenities have beckoned to the rehabilitation process. In turn, some newer structures—for instance in the crisis area of Brownsville in Brooklyn—began to deteriorate almost as soon as they were constructed in the 1940s. They are now abandoned or burned out shells.

A trip from southern Manhattan outward through the surrounding boroughs to the suburban counties is, to a large measure, a trip through time. At the point on the Lower East Side of Manhattan near the Chinese district of Chatham Square we find vestiges of what used to be numerous streets of Old Law tenements in the 1870s. Earlier housing tended to lack light and ventilation in interior rooms. The Tenement Act of 1867 required the plan of the tenement to be dumbell shaped, in order to provide airshafts at the waist of the building. Many of these structures still exist along Madison, Catherine, and Henry streets in the Lower East Side. Because late nineteenth century subway construction proceeded northward in Manhattan and eastward through Brooklyn, districts of Old Law tenements to this day are scattered along the rights of way of several branches of the Interborough Rapid Transit (IRT) and Brooklyn and Manhattan Transit (BMT).

By 1904 transit had reached northward into Harlem and its extension in the Bronx and Brooklyn was well under way. Thus northern Manhattan, especially the Broadway line of the IRT, and portions of the South Bronx become the *loci classici* of the New Law tenement. These structures are usually larger than the Old Law tenements and have more front footage. Rooms are more spacious and they were required to be designed to higher sanitary stan-

dards. Decorative touches such as white stone corner quoins against a red brick base and matching stone treatment of window lintels and sills, sometimes with egg and dart embellishments, are frequently found. The best of these buildings are valued as residences, especially in the neighborhood of Columbia University, owing to the excellent interior plaster work and fireplaces. Many have, of course, fallen into desuetude, as have the bulk of the Old Laws.

Most of the post-1929, yet pre–World War II buildings are concentrated in the more outlying reaches of the older boroughs and in Queens and Staten Island. Since World War II, however, the profitability of high-rise, high rental apartments of few rooms catering to singles or childless couples has led to a renewal cycle of inner city construction. Especially along the East Side of Manhattan, north of the midtown office district, new construction appears among the Old and New Law structures of York, First, and Second avenues, breaking up the integrity of the old German-American Yorkville area. Development south of midtown, already starting, is triggered to explode if and when the new Second Avenue subway is further along in construction, an eventuality which has recently been cast into doubt since work was indefinitely suspended as a result of the 1975 city fiscal crisis.

TENANTRY

The black population of New York is quite heterogeneous. Many recent black immigrants are persons of urban American origin, whereas earlier migrants came from the rural South. There are enclaves of West Indian blacks in Har-

Table 4. New York City Household Heads, by Race and Ethnic Group, 1970 (percent)

Borough	Non-Puerto Rican		Puerto Rican	Other	Total	Total Households (1,000s)
	White	*Negro*				
Bronx	55	21	14	10	100	497
Brooklyn	66	21	7	6	100	876
Manhattan	65	19	8	8	100	687
Queens	81	10	1	8	100	690
Richmond	90	4	1	4	100	86
All Households	68	17	7	8	100	2,837

Source: U.S. Bureau of the Census, 1970 Census of Population.

lem and elsewhere that lend additional diversity to the scene—the blocks to the west of Mount Morris Park (with St. Martin's Episcopal Church as a cultural focus) contain many middle class blacks of West Indian origin, areas in Queens are inhabited by French-speaking Haitians, and there is a Cape Verdean League in Harlem. The census category "black" in the New York case implies much more ethnic and cultural diversity compared to other American cities.

What holds true for blacks is also true of "Puerto Ricans." The visitor to the Chelsea district of Manhattan (West Side in the teens and twenties) may discover that some of the persons of Spanish surname who are sometimes labeled "Puerto Rican" are republican refugees from the Spanish Civil War, who sometimes entered the U.S. via Puerto Rico. Dominicans, Cubans, and many other persons of Hispanic origin form mixed families with Puerto Ricans and are sometimes misclassified. As a result, the significance of the term "Puerto Rican" is somewhat doubtful.

Queens and Richmond are the whitest (and most suburban) of the boroughs (Table 4). About 20 percent of the population of Manhattan, the Bronx, and Brooklyn are black (Figure 12). The Harlem concentration in central Manhattan is the best known of the black areas nationally. Central Brooklyn (Bedford-Stuyvesant) and its adjacent areas are even more extensive regions of concentrated black residency, however. That part of the South and East Bronx connected to the Harlem area by bridges across the Harlem River also contains a marked concentration of black residents.

Areas of Puerto Rican residence often lie between black areas and predominantly white ones (Figure 13). Thus, the Barrio (the East

Harlem Puerto Rican neighborhood) lies between Harlem and fashionable Park Avenue to the south. Between Bedford-Stuyvesant in Central Brooklyn, and white residential areas like the region from Flatlands to Bay Ridge to the south, there are Puerto Rican districts. A similar phenomenon is to be found in the Bronx, where Puerto Rican population concentrations in the Hunt's Point area lie between whites to the north and blacks to the southwest.

Insofar as tendencies may legitimately be observed among New York City's renters, blacks and Puerto Ricans tend to have larger, younger, and poorer families than whites. Black, Puerto Rican, and white families in descending order tend to have families with a female head (43.4, 33, and 31.3 percent, respectively).

In 1970, about 36 percent of white renter households had incomes below $6,000, while 39 percent had incomes above $10,000. For blacks, 52 percent of renter households had income below $6,000, while only about 19 percent had incomes in excess of $10,000. In the case of Puerto Ricans, 61 percent of renter households fell below $6,000, while only about 13 percent earned in excess of $10,000.

New York renters requiring the most in services, housing space, and access to mass transit inhabit the regions in Manhattan, the Bronx, and Brooklyn with the oldest housing stock (New and Old Law tenements). These houses are the costliest to maintain and renovate and possess the most obsolescent sanitary, electrical, plumbing, and heating systems. Moreover, there is a shortage of housing for the poor, since construction of low income housing has been far outstripped by demolition in favor

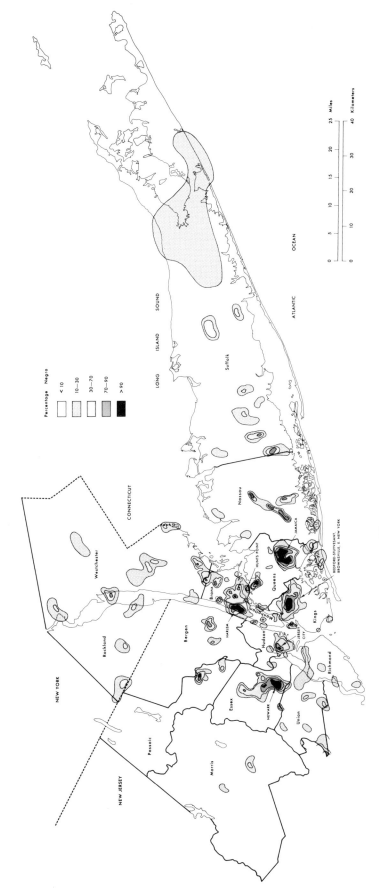

Figure 12. Map of Percentage Black.

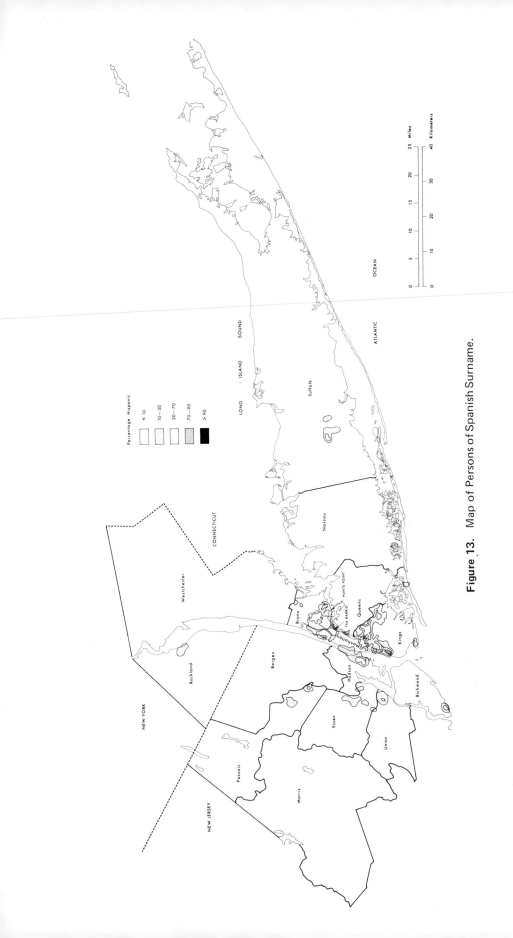

Figure 13. Map of Persons of Spanish Surname.

of the construction of high-rise, high rental units.

Recipients of public assistance live in housing badly in need of public or private rehabilitation, but for which no such assistance is forthcoming. Sternlieb estimates that more than 20 percent of Old Law and intermediate-sized New Law structures have over 20 percent of their tenants on welfare. The result is the kind of disaster which the reader who tours Brooklyn will witness in the Brownsville-East New York area—acres of rubble and demolished shells of hopeless buildings with blocks of tenements interspersed and an agonizing lag in new construction.

OWNERSHIP

There is a myth which pervades discussions of urban housing. It is that of the vicious slumlord whose vast domains of squalid tenements provide him with the means for squeezing profits out of the poor. From this follows an instant resolution of the housing problem: Let the slumlord be made to pay for the solution of the housing crisis. That imperative would be a fine policy statement if slumlords existed. Sadly enough—in the sense that it would simplify the solution—they do not.

Among the smaller Old Law and New Law tenements—housing New York's poorest tenants and creating the most acute problems in the city's housing stock—nearly 40 percent are in the hands of owners who own no other real estate. Only 16 to 20 percent of these categories are estimated to be in the hands of owners who own more than seven parcels. The large slumlord appears to be a myth.

In fact, most slum property owners in the city tend to follow a profession besides real estate as their primary occupation. In the poorest housing, more than 50 percent report their property income as a minor supplement to their regular income. These people tend to be craftsmen, workers, small businessmen, or retired people rather than real estate professionals or lawyers. In areas of the city where the tenantry is black or Puerto Rican, there is a concomitant tendency for the parcel owner to be black or Puerto Rican. An estimated 15 to 16 percent of the smaller Old and New Law tenements are owned by Spanish-speaking or non white owners. These are concentrated in districts of comparable tenantry. The owners tend to be newcomers to real estate ownership. This suggests that the least profitable real estate in the city is coming into the hands of inexperienced minority group ownership. The problems are obvious.

It is well to point out another form of ownership at this point—the city itself. In earlier days, when renewal or redevelopment of an area was contemplated, speculators would rush in and buy up parcels. Then, through paper transactions, they would bid up the apparent value of the parcel considerably, reaping windfall profits after condemnation. To correct this, the city passed "quick take" laws which can freeze the titles and status of all parcels in a redevelopment area, transferring title to the city and blocking speculative activity.

Unfortunately, this leaves the city as the owner of a number of decrepit buildings. Since the lag between condemnation and demolition may be years, and the city has not developed the funding necessary for adequate maintenance and service of these properties, and since there are few residential alternatives available to the occupants, the city finds itself as the landlord of these doomed and hopeless parcels. The social consequences to the children of a household living on a marginal level of public assistance who grow up in a squalid submarginal building that they perceive as being owned by the city may be imagined. They are prone to view the city as the oppressor that is forcing them to live in squalor, fear, and misery. Hostility to the landlord is transferred to the city and by extension to the political process. Alienation and anger are the result.

Condominiums and cooperatives are now put forward as solutions at least to the middle class need for housing. The more cynical note that transforming a multiple dwelling into a cooperative is a way for the owner to get out from under ownership and to pass on to the tenant-buyer the backbreaking maintenance and financing arrangements of the building. In return, the tenants receive ownership of an apartment which they might never be able to resell. Under these circumstances it is not remarkable that sales and transfers of coop apartments have recently become quite difficult.

Financing

A landlord usually requires mortgaging in order to acquire his property. His future success depends on resale value and the potential for remortgaging. Equity in the property is meaningless unless it can be recovered in cash. Remortgaging is one way of doing this. As a mortgage is paid off, the owner's wealth is held in real estate instead of cash. In an upward market, the owner may want to remortgage and translate his wealth into cash. Sale of the property is another way of doing this. Remortgaging in an upward market is analogous to sale to oneself using bank financing.

Sternlieb's study showed that 54 percent of owners of all the buildings considered in his research (including post-1929s) felt that if they could get institutional mortgage money on their properties (and many Old and New Law owners felt that they could not under any circumstances), they would have to supplement it with money out of their own resources. Sternlieb's conclusion: "In sum, many buildings have fallen out of the effective scope of the institutional money market" (p. 385). In other words, financial institutions had laid down a policy against lending on Old and New Law buildings regardless of condition. Furthermore, for the small Old and New Law tenements which form the heart of the poverty housing problem, the key reason for mortgage unavailability is their location. Insurance coverage is also difficult to get for these buildings. The mortgage and insurance company policies reinforce each other and present both the landlord and tenant with an impasse.

Under these circumstances, owner and tenant alike are ruined. How is the owner to maintain his obsolescent parcel in livable condition in the absence of financial incentives and in a neighborhood where the charging of higher rent is impossible? Tenants and prospective tenants cannot pay more either because of poverty or public assistance rigidities. Diverting any income at all to his personal benefit implies deterioration of his property and a decline in the quality of his tenantry. The point is often reached where the property is a drain on the owner. When efforts to sell are fruitless, abandonment starts to spread into the worst of these older borough areas.

Rent control is often blamed for the problem. Without a doubt the rigidities imposed by rent control upon the ability of rents to move upward affect the economics of many housing areas in the city. But, with respect to the question of poverty housing, abandonment, and the decay of neighborhoods that is so poignant in those areas inhabited by a young, minority, and public assistance clientele, it is doubtful whether rent control has much effect. After all, within the New York–New Jersey metropolitan region lies the major city of Newark, lacking rent control but acutely manifesting the same syndrome noticeable in the housing market of New York City. The hapless landlord, caught outside the mainstream of the real estate market, is rendered impotent by the deterioration of the neighborhood around him, mounting costs, and a limited flow of cash.

REHABILITATION—THE CLOGGING UP OF FILTERING DOWN

But let us renovate and rehabilitate the declining structures and thus upgrade the basic housing stock. Or else, let us build for the rich in confidence that an improved housing stock will "filter down" to the poor.

Brooklyn Heights stands as a splendid example of rehabilitation. Some areas of the city have intrinsic amenities—a well-scaled street plan, a noble view of a park or of the harbor; a supply of old and decaying yet architecturally distinctive brownstone townhouses which are cheap, subdivided, downgraded, but salvageable; access to centers of employment and shopping. Brooklyn Heights has them all. To a lesser degree, so do the nearby districts of Cobble Hill, Boerum Heights, Park Slope, and Fort Greene. A process begins in such a neighborhood which in New York City is called "brownstoning." People of means purchase and renovate the old brownstone townhouses, usually reserving one or two floors for themselves and developing flats on other floors for rental, at a good price. As the stroller through Brooklyn Heights will appreciate, the outcome is a charming, attractive neighborhood in which the essence of all that is best in a city is embodied.

The effect, however, is to displace a poor population (largely Syrian and Puerto Rican in the case of Cobble Hill, now in the midst of the process south of Brooklyn Heights) and to convert poor residences into wealthy ones. The "filtering" here is up, not down. Simultaneously, other poor neighborhoods are being "renewed."

Renewal generally involves the demolition of blocks which are suitable for "brownstoning" or renovation. Replacement is usually by high-rise buildings with small apartments at substantial rentals. Fifty or sixty years from now, if these buildings filter down, they will become instant slums if the poor tend to have families too large to be easily accommodated by the small apartments, as they do now. The immediate effect in renewal areas is to reduce the stock of housing for the poor. Tomkins Square, in the East Village, is at the center of an area which will be subject to demolition and rebuilding if the Second Avenue Subway is finished.

And then there are "cities within a city" or planned unit developments (PUDs). A PUD underway on Welfare Island in the East River includes 1,050 units, of which 20 percent are earmarked for low income families—a drop in the bucket.

The PUDs which are under construction in the NYMR will provide only a miniscule number of low income housing units in relation to the need revealed in the Brownsville and East New York area of demolition and condemnation. None of these solutions to the problems of urban housing is anywhere near to dealing with the scale of low income housing need.

Public low income housing developments have been slow in developing since federal funds have become less available and many critics have condemned them as unsatisfactory. New York City has still to devise a way to house the inhabitants of slums of despair such as those in these desolate areas of central Brooklyn.

Urban Landscapes and Social Processes

The history of European settlement of the New York Metropolitan Region spans the years from 1625 to the present. During those years, the landscape has been progressively transformed from a wooded archipelago inhabited by American Indians residing at low densities to an urbanized area in which great expanses of land have been paved over, filled in, and converted into a landscape of human artifice. In this landscape vestiges from earlier times may often be noted, and the nature of social processes related to their placement and use may be clarified. As the geologist reads events relating to the history of the earth from layers of sediment deposited in earlier eras, the artifacts present in an urban neighborhood can help us recreate social processes of bygone days. There are several such in the New York Metropolitan Region.

THE WALL STREET-BATTERY AREA OF SOUTHERN MANHATTAN

Little remains of the Dutch and early English colonial eras in New York City, although there are some early Dutch farmhouses in New Jersey, a few old houses on Long Island, and one schoolhouse from the seventeenth century in Staten Island. The street layout of the Wall Street area, however, is from the past. Broad Street and Beaver Street, at the core of the financial district, were canals in the Dutch days. Many streets carry the name "slip" (Coenties Slip, Rutgers Slip, Peck Slip). A slip was the channel of water between two finger piers. In effect these streets were originally water channels along which the Dutch and English merchants did their business, for southern Manhattan was originally a group of islands in a maze of marshy channels.

The present shoreline of the East River has been extended several hundred feet from the original shoreline which lay near Water Street (now far inland). Part of the shoreline extension has to do with the fact that sanitary wastes, offal, and refuse were commonly dumped into the slips until navigation was impossible. Then landfill was added and new finger piers were built farther out into the river. The process then began again.

Fraunces Tavern is a much renovated 1719 building still standing in the area. Famous as the site of Washington's farewell address, it serves to make a useful social point. The proprietor, Black Sam Fraunces, was Washington's victualer, and became a member of the free black community in the city after the Revolution. Much of the restaurant, catering, and related industries in Manhattan during the first half of the nineteenth century was carried on by free Negro entrepreneurs. This was not atypical. W.E.B. DuBois, in his 1899 study, *The Philadelphia Negro,* alludes to the League of Negro Caterers as an established organization in eastern cities.

The great fire of 1835 devastated the Wall Street area, and what conflagration failed to do, real estate development accomplished, so that only a couple of blocks of 1811–1850 buildings are left in the South Street Seaport Restora-

Figure 14.   Schermerhorn Row. These buildings date variously from 1811 to 1850.

tion area (Figure 14). These do, however, indicate that until the midnineteenth century, and during the heyday of the clipper ship, it was the East River side of lower Manhattan which was the seaport and not the Hudson River side. A glance at a regional map will show that the East River communicates not only with lower New York Bay, the Atlantic Ocean, and southern coastal routes, but also with New England via Long Island Sound. India House, a stately 1854 building was a center for midcentury commercial activity (Figure 15).

The northern boundary of the district on the East Side is the stately Brooklyn Bridge (1883) built by the Roeblings. Its location and date are also of some significance. By 1883, both Brooklyn (then a separate city) and New York were rapidly urbanizing and interdependent entities. The ward of New York north of the bridge had a density exceeding 300,000 per square mile. When technology developed to the point where a bridge was feasible, it was so located as to

link the City Hall of New York with its Brooklyn counterpart.

CHATHAM SQUARE

The Chatham Square region, to the north of the Brooklyn Bridge, is an extremely rich and complex one. Owing to the convergence of a number of streets into a square, which was once called "Paradise Square," it has also been called the "Five Points."

The earliest artifact in this area is the Congregation Shearith Israel burying ground (1682), located on the Bowery, which was then a rural farm-to-market road (Figure 16). Note the land level of the cemetery in relation to the surroundings as an indication of landscape change.

By 1820, the area had passed from rural to suburban (Figure 17). By 1840 many squalid pre-Old Law tenements had been built signaling the transition of the area to a poor core city slum inhabited largely by Irish immigrants. Demolition and intensive building occurred

Figure 15. India House on Hanover Square, an 1854 commercial building located near where Captain Kidd (a distinguished vestryman of Trinity Church) had his residence earlier.

Figure 16. Shearith Israel Burying Ground (1682) which reveals the early land level near Chatham Square.

Figure 17. Early townhouses built during the urbanization of the Chatham Square-Five Points Area, circa 1822.

during the 1870s and 1880s, resulting in block after block of Old Law tenements housing the poor Italian and Jewish immigrants who labored in the city's growing garment trades and construction trades (Figure 18).

The modern American can have little grasp of what it was like to live in this district in the nineteenth century. Until 1842, the poor New Yorker had to depend on well water (the first aqueduct brought fresh water to the city only in 1842). In the Chatham Square area a marshy site called the Collect Pond, which had originally been a small lake before it became choked with refuse, was the principal source. Now completely filled in and converted into the site of the Criminal Courts Buildings and a park, it was then highly polluted. Typhus, typhoid, yellow fever, and cholera periodically ravaged the district. Matter from a neaby potter's field leached into the groundwater after mass burials until 1827 when burials south of Grand Street were prohibited. In 1840 one person in four died in this area, yet the plague of 1849 was reputed to have been more serious.

We are now in a position to note that the suburban phase (Georgian and Greek Revival townhouses), gave way to the old Five Points phase (pre-1867 tenements) and thence to the Old Law tenement phase, and finally to the Chinese district of today.

Corresponding to the first phase were "old Knickerbocker" family groups. After the Napoleonic Wars and the distress in English industrial districts which led to the Peterloo Massacre of 1819, the fringes of the area were occupied by poor English immigrants. Notorious and vicious gangs which included English youths ravaged the Five Points. These gave way, in turn, to the Irish and German migrants of the 1840s and 1850s. The "Dead Rabbits," Roach Guards, and Kerryownians terrorized New York until the 1860s when gang activity peaked in connection with the draft riots of 1863.

Corresponding to the Old Law tenement phase was the development of the Jewish and Italian Lower East Side pattern. Between the Bowery and the East River was Jewish turf (centered upon East Broadway). West of the

Figure 18. Old Law Tenement in Chatham Square District. Notice the indentations on the side which, together with matching ones on an adjoining building, provided an airshaft for fenestration. The adjoining building predates the Old Tenement Law of 1867.

Bowery was Italian turf (centered upon Mulberry Street). The Bowery was no man's land—a dark and dangerous place covered by an elevated rapid transit railroad. The song "The Bowery," with its refrain, "I'll never go there any more," sums it up.

Not until the years immediately preceding the First World War did the Chinese move into the area as still later occupants of the shabby and variegated housing stock of the area. Again crime flared up briefly. The Hip Sing and On Leong tongs fought for control of the district along Mott and Pell streets and in the "bloody angle" of Doyer Street.

Vestiges of the Italian period may still be seen on Mulberry Street, in the form of funeral parlors with Italian names which are still available to cater to the needs of the last of the previous population wave. Manhattan Bridge, however, and its landward extension, Canal Street, have become the rough boundary of the Chinese area to the south and the Italian and formerly Jewish, but now largely Hispanic, areas to the north.

In the early part of the nineteenth century, the workers from the Irish slums walked south to the old East River waterfront to work. By the Old Law tenement phase, jobs were located to the northwest in Manhattan's interior where the Cast Iron District was being built to house the growing needle trades industries of the city.

THE LOWER EAST SIDE

North of Canal Street and west of the Bowery lies the old Italian Lower East Side, which preserves much of its ethnic identity to this day, while the Jewish Lower East Side, east of the Bowery, has changed substantially. In the Italian district, Italian tricolor streamers and painted fire hydrants in red, white, and green are noted everywhere. Even when the younger generation of Italian-American families moves to a suburban residence, it is often a matter of routine for them to return regularly to the old Italian East Side to visit with relatives. On such occasions as the feast of San Gennaro, during the week of September 19, the streets are packed with vendors selling delicacies and throngs of revelers.

Grand Street, in the northern portion of the Italian district, is still noted for fine Italian needlework (Figure 19). A declining bridal gown industry is still located there. Italian-

American citizens concerned with preservation are now mounting an effort to preserve this ethnic neighborhood as an historic area.

In contrast, there has been much change in the Jewish Lower East Side. Demolition of the Old Law stock has been extensive, as more modern housing has been underwritten by the activities of such unions as the International Ladies Garment Workers' Union. This has led to the establishment of a well-housed population with dependable purchasing power in the area (Figure 20). Symptomatic of this, there has been some commercial improvement in areas near the union housing.

A social landmark in the area is the Henry Street Settlement. Established by Lillian Wald in 1893, it is famous in the annals of social reform (Figure 21). It occupies beautiful restored Greek revival townhouses of the 1827–34 period. To the south of the settlement, however, lies its problem and a challenge. Signs with Hebrew characters confront streets with Hispanic pedestrians.

This is an area in which an aging and declining Jewish population is being replaced by a young, predominantly Catholic Puerto Rican population. The settlement houses are left without the population to serve for which they were intended. The newcomers, badly in need of service, have not found the avenue by which assistance might flow to them from the agencies. It is a dilemma of neighborhood change.

Yet there is still one landscape element left which evokes the old Jewish Lower East Side most forcefully. On Sunday, the outdoor market on Orchard Street still teems with activity and with bargainseekers from all over the metropolis (Figure 22).

THE CAST IRON DISTRICT

The heart of the city's early garment industry, toward which many of the inhabitants of Five Points and the Lower East Side turned for employment in the 1870s and 1880s, is also an architectural treasure. South of Houston Street (always pronounced How-stun in New York) lies the district called SoHo. Along such thoroughfares as Greene Street lie some of the finest examples of the cast iron factory loft style of construction which the city possesses (Figure 23). Following the renown of such efforts as the Crystal Palace in London (1851) which employed cast iron, New York designers such as

Figure 19. Bridal Goods Shop on Grand Street near the Bowery.

Figure 20. The Sidney Hillman Homes (1926-1930). Financed by the Amalgamated Clothing Workers, these houses replaced primarily Old Law and pre-Old Law dwellings.

Figure 21. The fine old 1827–1834 townhouses occupied by the Henry Street Settlement, the principal of which is shown here, have been carefully preserved and restored.

Bogardus, Gaynor, Thomas, Fernback, and Snook developed a style in which entire facades were cast in units which were decorated in classical ornaments.

Today, the person standing on Greene Street and Grand looking north can recapture the 1870 factory loft cityscape to a great degree, for the entire district is still nearly intact. Obsolescent for factory use, these lofts have attracted attention as workplace-residences. In fact, near Houston Street it is noticeable how many of the cast iron lofts are being lived in.

Strictly speaking, such occupancy is illegal in New York. If, however, a person claims that he is operating a residence-workshop in an activity which requires loft space, he can be permitted to do so. Many artists have taken advantage of this provision and an art-oriented neighborhood is developing there. This is quite in conformity with the tradition of Greenwich Village, immediately north of Houston Street.

In 1875, the workers in a SoHo loft would walk westward to their jobs from the Lower East Side. Some of the affluent owners and

Figure 22. The rich and diversified ethnic mix of the Lower East Side is manifested in this Sunday photograph of the Orchard Street Market.

managers of lofts would journey south to their places of business from their fashionable Greenwich Village or Chelsea townhouses. The pattern is not unlike that in which, today, core city workers are separated in residence from the suburban white collar and professional classes by a perimeter factory belt.

Yet, as the lovely tree-shaded streets of Greenwich Village declined at the end of the nineteenth century, it became a poor neighborhood of tenements and cheap rooming houses carved out of declining townhouses (Figure 24). After World War I, artists popularized residence here. These "bohemians" alerted the otherwise insensitive public to the intrinsic worth of the Village as an attractive cityscape. Redevelopment drove out the artists as land values boomed.

Moving due east, toward the river, artists next invaded the East Village. In the years after World War II, the cycle repeated itself. Now the commercialized bohemia of the East Village has again priced them out of the market. In lieu of

moving directly into the river, the next shift was to SoHo. As the reader may already have guessed, cast iron loft space is rapidly getting priced out of sight. Thus, the poor artist creates the very condition which drives him from the district which he has had the vision to renew.

THE BARRIO

Park Avenue is a synonym for wealth. From 42nd Street to 96th Street along this boulevard lie fifty blocks of housing for the wealthy. Yet at 96th Street a remarkable transition occurs (Figure 25). A sharp downslope in the road grade results in the Penn Central tracks emerging above ground upon an embankment. Immediately the landscape changes to one of poverty. Within only one block, comfortable, well-kept New Law structures give way to decaying Old Law tenements, run-down townhouses, and public housing developments. This

Figure 23. The Haughwout Building (1857) at Broome Street and Broadway. Its cast iron exterior by J. P. Gaynor, early date of construction, and pioneering interior elevator by E. G. Otis make it a landmark. Most of its cast iron neighbors in this portion of the district, however, are later in date (1870–1890).

Figure 24. An Urban Miniature Landscape. Barrow Street townhouses, circa 1826–1828, in Greenwich Village.

is the Barrio. It is a powerful demonstration of how landform influences cityscape.

To the right of the "Chinese Wall" of the railroad rampart lies the vast tract which James Delano sold to the city in 1825 for $25,000. The completion of subway lines such as the Lenox Avenue (1904) during the turn of the century period opened up Harlem to settlement.

The area now known as Spanish Harlem was at first Italian. Suburban central Harlem was the subject of extensive fashionable townhouse development in the 1880s and 1890s. The poorer Italians were crammed into the East Harlem fringes. By the 1920s, however, there were also some good blocks of well-to-do Italians mixed in with the tenement dwellers. Slowly in the 1940s, and then rapidly following the Second World War, as the younger generations of Italians left for the suburbs, poor young Puerto Rican families began to fill in the vacancies. Today, the area has become Hispanic.

A central institution in Spanish Harlem is La Marqueta, the Spanish Market, which occupies space under the Penn Central railroad tracks along Park Avenue from 112th to 116th streets. Inside the shed buildings of the market, the ambience of shopping crowds, odors, sights of tropical vegetable products, and spoken Spanish is unforgettable. Prices are good, and since it is a New York City market, quality is supervised. One may purchase avocados, mangos, bananas, plantains, yautia, names, sofrito, and achiote seed among other things. So attractive is the market to business, that along 116th Street and Park Avenue it has spilled over into sidewalk stalls.

HARLEM

The suburbanization of the rural fringe village of Harlem ‡ates from the 1880s, when townhouses were constructed there. But the suburban phase did not last long, as a depression combined with a softening of the real estate

(A)

(B)

Figure 25. **(A)** Park Avenue and 96th Street Looking South. A landscaped median mall contributes to the scale of the apartment buildings of the wealthy. **(B)** Same Location Looking North. The emergence of the New York Central tracks blights a landscape of Old and New Law tenements and public housing projects.

market to produce a condition of overbuilding in Harlem (Figure 26). These circumstances, combined with the destruction of an earlier site of the black community for the purpose of building Pennsylvania Station led to the entrance of blacks into the portions of Harlem north of 130th Street.

Until about 1930, Harlem south of 125th Street and west of Fifth Avenue was Jewish (Figure 27). In fact, Italian Harlem and Jewish Harlem existed side by side as the turfs of the two groups had in the Lower East Side, except that now the Italians were nearer the river.

Change occurred swiftly in the 1930s, however, and black Harlem now extends all the way to Central Park. One can still notice signs of former times on the Mount Olivet Baptist Church at Lenox Avenue near 125th Street (Figure 28). Originally the Temple Israel, it still has the Star of David on the windows. It now lies near the Muslim Mosque at which Malcolm X preached (Figure 29).

Two neighborhoods of Harlem will serve to dispel the myth that this complex residential area is an undifferentiated black slum. Mount Morris Park near St. Martin's Church represents an area inhabited by many West Indian blacks who have preserved a middle class atmosphere to the west of the park where in the summer events of the Harlem Cultural Festival take place.

The second neighborhood lies around 135th Street and Lenox Avenue. The landscape here includes Harlem Hospital, several developments of black cooperative high quality housing, and the Shomburg Branch of the New York Public Library renowned for its collection of American black historical documents.

One Hundred Thirty-Fifth Street is close to being a central focus of intellectual life in Harlem (Figure 30). Nearby are the Harlem YMCA and the Abyssinian Baptist Church, central cultural institutions. Most of the apartment buildings here were built after the New Tenement Law of 1901 (Figure 31).

Between 138th and 139th streets and Seventh and Eighth avenues is a New York historical landmark—the block of houses along 138th

Figure 26. Harlem Brownstone Townhouses circa 1890 Flank St. Martin's Church (1888). The church serves a West Indian congregation, many of whom live nearby.

Figure 27. Astor Row. Downgraded townhouses circa 1890 on West 130th near Lenox Avenue. The amiable young man asked whether I would take his picture as he took mine!

and 139th streets some of which were designed by Stamford White and built by McKim, Mead and White in 1903. A walk along the row on 139th Street especially gives one a sense of the quiet scale and quality of these buildings. Here, as well as in the Mount Morris area and elsewhere in Harlem, black families of means have "brownstoned" and retored many of the houses, as whites have done in Brooklyn.

The Paul Lawrence Dunbar Apartments (1928), nearby, were designed by Andrew J. Thomas, a prize-winning effort. The landscaped inner court is a pleasant and peaceful place to walk through. From the outset, designed as a residence for blacks, many of the present cultural and political leaders of Harlem have lived there.

Visitors to Harlem will appreciate the complex texture of the area. Some good and much poor housing exist close together. Poverty areas adjoin neighborhoods which manifest means and taste. The ethnic diversity of the popula-

tion is reflected in their cultural and religious institutions. It does not lend itself to facile stereotype.

BROOKLYN HEIGHTS

Like Greenwich Village, Brooklyn Heights is a community where site, situation, and development history have combined to produce an urban district rich in amenities. One need only walk along the Esplanade (completed in 1950–1951) at the foot of Montague Street to realize that nowhere else in the NYMR is there a better view of the towers of Wall Street, the old harbor area, and the Brooklyn Bridge. (Figure 32). As early as the 1830s, sail and steam ferries made commutation between this location and lower New York feasible and pleasant, while the shopping center and city hall area of the city of Brooklyn was developing only a few blocks inland.

Figure 28. Mount Olivet Baptist Church, Lenox Avenue, Harlem (1907). The Star of David may be distinguished in the upper arch of the windows recalling its previous role as the Temple Israel of Harlem.

Whole blocks of the suburbs of 1830 to 1850 remain in this charming tree-lined locale. The portion of the Heights nearest to the Esplanade was developed as a splendid pedestrian court lined with townhouses (Montague Terrace and Pierrepoint Place, 1857–1886) in which Abiel Low and his son Seth Low lived (Figure 33). Seth Low was one of the first mayors of the combined city of New York and Brooklyn under the consolidation of 1898.

While, in the course of time, outlying streets at some remove from this central point became run down and subdivided into rooming houses, the Montague Terrace location retained its urbane charm and quiet luster. Yet even some of the tenements built at the outskirts of the Heights were distinctive. The Tower and Home Apartments (1878–1879) were built as model tenements for the poor with the aid of philanthropist Alfred Tredway (Figure 34).

Considering that they were contemporary with the Old Law tenements of Manhattan, they are a constructive innovation, embodying better ventilation. There is an open yard behind the apartments which provides through ventilation. Warren Place, a few steps to the east, is a gem (Figure 35). A walk through this charming court invites one to inspect the workmen's cottages built as a part of the same development. The *AIA Guide* by Norval White and Elliot Wilensky tells us that these six-room cottages rented for $18 per month. The four room apartments in the tenement rented for $1.93 per week. This was one of the first low rent "projects" in New York which was much emulated in Northern Europe, if not in the United States. Are the most recent ones much of an improvement?

With the decline of the southern and eastern fringes of the Heights in the early twentieth century, a Near Eastern population came to occupy many of the old houses. One can still see an occasional Syrian shop along Atlantic Avenue (Figure 36). More recently, a Hispanic

Figure 29. This Muslim Mosque near Lenox Avenue and 117th Street has become the focus for Muslim-related social activities. Malcom X was its most distinguished founder. It typifies the diversity and complex texture of Harlem.

Figure 30. This Harlem cooperative, with integrated shopping, has replaced older structures at Lenox and 135th Street. Across the street from Harlem Hospital and near cultural centers, it is a sought-after residential complex.

population of predominantly Puerto Rican origin has established residence in the downgraded townhouses of the Heights and adjoining Cobble Hill.

But a countervailing tendency has manifested itself. The intrinsic amenities of the Heights, sharpened by housing shortages, has led people with means and with a taste for urban life to purchase downgraded old townhouses with their stately brownstone facades, interior fireplaces, high ceilings, and fine plaster work. The poor residents are evicted and the places rehabilitated into spacious, floor through apartments, with the proud owner living in a ground floor duplex with a backyard garden. This process, called "brownstoning," amounts to the replacement of a dense, poor population with a less dense affluent one.

Almost all of the Heights north of Atlantic Avenue has been thus "unslummed" (Jane Jacobs' striking term). The process is now spreading to the southeast, displacing Syrian

and Puerto Rican families. The net result is to erode further the number of housing units available to the poor, as described in the preceding section.

BROWNSVILLE-EAST NEW YORK

There is a neighborhood in Brooklyn known as Brownsville and East New York which, until the end of World War II, was largely composed of Jewish lower middle class residents. Today, this population has mostly been replaced by an extremely poor population, largely on public assistance, composed primarily of minority groups. The neighborhood change was facilitated by the entrance of the Bedford-Stuyvesant and Bushwick populations from the north and west, and by the location of major highrise low income housing projects in the heart of Brownsville.

In the midst of a neighborhood diminishing in economic status and purchasing power, com-

Figure 31. A New Law tenement (post-1901) on the corner with Beaux-Arts-style trim and characteristic ground floor shops. The white building adjoining is the Shomburg Library (1905). Harlem: Lenox Avenue and 135th Street.

Figure 32. Lower Manhattan from the Montague Street Esplanade, Brooklyn Heights. The East River is in the foreground. Out of the picture, to the left, lie Upper and Lower New York Bay, and the harbor entrance.

Figure 33. The Low House, Brooklyn Heights. A townhouse row in the background. To the right, a fine Beaux-Arts-style New Law building.

mercial blight and business property vacancies abound. The 1970 mean family income here was about $6,500, with much public assistance. Maintenance and operative costs have risen, accompanied by the decline of income and purchasing power in the neighborhood. The result is a region of desperation. The landlord and tenant, usually of different racial and ethnic origin, become pitted against one another. The landlord sees his property investment vanishing. The tenant sees the rapid erosion of quality in his residence. The hostility between the two, nurtured by the economic crunch, leads to abandonment on the part of the landlord, and squatting and rent strikes on the part of the tenants.

The city has entered the Brownsville-East New York area with a major Model Cities program. Construction under the program has failed to keep pace with demolitions, however, and some families have been temporarily placed in trailers, while others live in condemned houses awaiting demolition and owned by the city (Figure 37). The scope of the problem,

when measured against the efficacy of available solutions, presents a gloomy picture (Figure 38).

THE PATERSON-FAIR LAWN, NEW JERSEY, REGION*

Paterson, New Jersey, was one of the cradles of the American industrial revolution. The mill district clustered around the Great Falls contains valuable archeological remnants of early industrial buildings and hydraulic works. The Great Falls Development Corporation, a nonprofit, public membership organization, has set for itself the commendable task of working to

*The author is indebted to the Great Falls Development Corporation and the Society for Industrial Archaeology, both of Paterson, for much of the information contained in this section, which has been made available to me through their kind cooperation. Materials on the Riverside District in Paterson may be secured by writing to Great Falls Development Corporation, Maple Street, Great Falls Park, Paterson, New Jersey 07502.

Figure 34. The Tower and Home Apartments, Brooklyn.

Figure 35. Warren Place, Next Door to the Tower and Home. These cottages, originally built for the poor, are now much in demand. Will modern model low income housing of today be in demand in 2075?

Figure 36. Near Eastern Shops on Atlantic Avenue, Brooklyn. Notice the Arabic lettering on the sign at the left. The buildings are nineteenth century townhouses, renovated. Note the Arabic characters displayed in a residential window in the upper left.

Figure 37. Temporary prefabricated trailer structures housing some of the families displaced by demolition, Brownsville, Brooklyn. In the background, the middle income developments have balconies, the lower income ones don't.

preserve this area as an historic urban industrial park.

The Great Falls area of Paterson was selected by Alexander Hamilton at the behest of our First Congress as a site where power, markets, labor, and raw materials could converge into a national manufactory. The Society for Establishing Useful Manufacture (SUM) was created to administer and promote its development. Pierre L'Enfant, of Washington, D.C., fame, was engaged to plan the district, but his grandoise design came to naught save the middle hydraulic race (Figure 39).

Peter Colt of Connecticut, one of a succession of Colts prominent in the district, assumed prominence in 1792 when he established a cotton-spinning mill. By 1816, protected by the tariff, Paterson grew rapidly in cotton textiles. Machine repair and foundry industries grew alongside the cotton mills.

The end of the 1830s saw the beginning of the silk boom, while the metalworking industries matured into locomotive manufacture.

The predominantly male labor force in locomotives and foundries was thus the complement to the female labor force in textiles. By the time of the Civil War, Paterson was America's leading locomotive producer.

Even though obsolescence and industrial strife in the shape of the tragic Silk Strike of 1913 took its toll on the district in the twentieth century, there continues to be a residue of textile manufacture in the old mills (Figure 40).

Adjoining Paterson on the opposite bank of the Passaic River is the suburb of Fair Lawn. A portion of Fair Lawn, called Radburn, is the location of a celebrated planned development by Henry Wright and Clarence Stein, distinguished "new town" planners of the pre–World War II era.

The houses in Radburn are developed on small plots clustered around cul-de-sac driveways which are arranged around the perimeter of large "superblocks." Thus, while neighbors are close together, and their driveways give

Figure 38. Demolition, Abandonment, and Condemnation in Brownsville, Brooklyn. All of the buildings to the right and center are empty. Some are burned out by vagrant fires. Most of the buildings at the right were built in the 1930s. Elsewhere in the city there are buildings of this style which remain in good condition. In the center background can be seen a middle income structure which will not solve the housing problems of the poor displaced in large numbers from demolished tenements. To the left, in the background, is part of a low income public housing project. Loss of low income housing has so far exceeded replacement in this area. There are literally acres of Brownsville which have resembled this photograph for more than five years.

auto access at the rear of the house, the front of the house faces upon the beautifully landscaped common parkland of the block interiors. A walk through the paths which penetrate the commons will show a variety of interesting touches. Sandboxes for children have been placed at frequent intervals. An occasional gazebo will be seen. The circulation pattern, emulating the pioneering work of Olmstad and Vaux in Central and Prospect parks, separates vehicular and pedestrian traffic completely (Figure 41). Where a path crosses a road, there is a tunnel for pedestrians. A common recreational facility including a pool and tennis courts has been built into the plan, as has an elementary school.

Originally conceived as a complete "garden city," the original plan provided for four times

the area actually developed, and intended to allocate space for commercial and industrial use so that workplace and residence might be brought together. Unfortunately, the stock market crash of 1929 and the ensuing disaster in the real estate industry aborted the scheme.

Yet, partially developed or not, these houses, which sold (more than forty years ago) at prices in the $10,000 range, have appreciated in value more than four times. The development's common land and facilities, which are managed by the nonprofit Radburn Corporation, are kept as a vital external amenity for the resident. The purchaser of a house automatically becomes a voting member of the corporation and agrees to pay an assessment (which has averaged less than $200 per year recently) to cover common expenses. Upon selling, the

Figure 39. The Upper Race which diverted water from the Upper Passaic River to the Mill District Patterson. Designed by Pierre L'Enfant.

sale passes through the corporation which maintains a listing of prospective buyers.

At first—although racial and religious restrictions were imposed—it was considered a goal to have a broad cross-section of economic classes represented among Radburn residents. As time went on, however, marginal owners were wiped out by the Depression, while property values appreciated. As a result, today Radburn is somewhat more skewed toward the higher socioeconomic categories than the founders intended. Developments like Radburn and Sunnyside should be studied carefully today, as PUDs and enterprises like Reston, Virginia, and Columbia, Maryland, are conceived to foster social goals in the mid-1970s similar to those the earlier developments intended to serve in 1927-1932, in the teeth of the processes of the land market. As in the case of Brooklyn Heights, we may wonder whether intrinsic good physical design may

not serve to defeat goals of socioeconomic heterogeneity as the price of scarce good physical design gets bid upward.

It is fascinating to notice how little influence Radburn has had upon its surroundings. If one were to leave Radburn along streets named for such pioneering planners as Ebenezer Howard, the boundary is sharp; one would see that typical suburban development houses cluster right upon its doorstep. The reason may also be partly understood in terms of our economic system.

Radburn was somewhat more expensive to build than neighboring areas of Fair Lawn and East Paterson (Figure 42). Since (under the concept of a limited profit development corporation) the house selling prices were to be kept competitive with these areas while fewer units were built per acre, at best, when sold, the Radburn houses would be less profitable to the builder than the others. Yet, if

Figure 40. Paterson Mill Building. The water flows through the lower race beneath the building. It used to be used for water wheels which provided factory power through a vertical arrangement of belts and pulleys. Textiles are still made in this building, using electric power.

(A)

(B)

Figure 41. Radburn. **(A)** Houses are clustered around automobile access cul-de-sacs. This frees the large block interiors for landscaping. **(B)** On the opposite side of the same houses, pedestrian walks communicate to the landscaped block interior. Pedestrian walkways are kept separate from automobile roads as an important design feature.

Figure 42. Radburn. **(A)** A pedestrian path avoids contact with an automobile road by means of an underpass. **(B)** Landscaped block interior with gazebo.

(C)

Figure 42, continued. Radburn. (C) Communal pool and children's recreation area in block interior.

total cost to society over the years is considered, many of the $10,000, 1929 Paterson bungalows are now valueless slums.

Profits of housing development are reaped by the seller at the time of the sale. Costs of shoddy layout and construction are paid by the buyer (or by society after downgrading and abandonment) long after the sale. In the short run shoddy practice yields higher individual profits to the builder, but in the long run greater social costs result. Except for the occasional idealist like Clarence Stein or Henry Wright there seems to be little profit incentive to create Radburns. Thus good design remains scarce, and gets bid up in price and taken out of the reach of the working class and poor family as the slum-generating and slum-concentrating processes of our economic system continue to operate, leaving interstitial oases of good design for the affluent.

The Urban Environment—The Pollution Feedback

Since the metropolis is a junction in the organization of our society at which energy, materials, people, and land are combined in the productive and distributive processes by which our needs are met, it follows that the metropolis is likewise the place at which the waste products from these processes are concentrated. Let us consider the ecological process which imposes stress upon the vital components of the NYMR environment—the land, water, and air. Metropolitan population growth stimulates in a complex way activities such as industry, retailing, and local service provision which are directed toward local consumption, as well as export and import activities which cross the region's boundary. The population growth occurs partly through natural increase and partly through inmigration related to employment expansion.

During expansion of economic activity and population, the demand for space in the metropolis intensifies, inducing environmental change. Direct demand for land and water is affected as waste generation leads to landfill on the one hand and pollution of water on the other. Scarce water reserves lead to the inundation and reduction of the land area supply in the form of reservoirs and storage facilities, while sanitary landfill shapes the growth of some parts of the region.

Eventually, environmental stress can lead to a brake on growth. High costs and few amenities pressure individuals into leaving. The affluent have the most options and tend to leave, while the weak and the poor, those with the least choice, will stay. Environmental stress has reached the New York metropolitan region.

WATER QUALITY AND THE NEW YORK-NEW JERSEY BIGHT

In the late nineteenth century, oyster fisheries were a principal industry in upper New York Bay, the Kill van Kull north of Staten Island, the Arthur Kill west of Staten Island, and Newark Bay (Figure 43). Today, the bottom of these waterways is simply dead muck filled with oyster shells. Water samples taken from the Kill van Kull have indicated that even coliform (intestinal) bacteria cannot survive in it. During the months of July and August, reaches of the Arthur Kill run septic, completely lacking in dissolved oxygen, it all having been consumed oxidizing organic waste. The impact of the petrochemical and other industries, and the sewage effluent generated by the New York-New Jersey metropolitan region, have been catastrophic.

Fortunately, while the estuary remains a disaster, progress has been made in cleaning up the Hudson River. As a result of the combined efforts of public enforcement agencies and conservation and sportsmen's groups, the Hudson River has sufficiently recovered in quality so that the annual shad migration north of the city has returned in force.

But other rivers are not so fortunate. The Passaic, flowing through Paterson, Passaic, and Newark, is indescribably contaminated, as is the lower Hackensack where it empties into the

Figure 43. Howland's Hook, Staten Island, New York. The Arthur Kill (middle distance) frequently runs septic (no dissolved oxygen) in the summer owing to pollution. Dump in the foreground, petroleum-based chemical industry in New Jersey (background). The air, water, and solid waste pollution problem flows across state lines.

tidal marshes across which the New Jersey Turnpike wends its way to New York City (Figure 44). In Dutch days these two rivers so abounded with salmon that the good burghers passed an ordinance forbidding landlords from relying exclusively on that fish to feed their indentured servants. As late as the turn of the twentieth century, the now foul tidal marsh area was a noted fishing, hunting, and trapping summer resort for the cities nearby.

But the pollution has not stopped at the estuary. Sewage sludge and other waste has for years been barged out into the Atlantic Ocean and dumped south of the Narrows (the passage between Brooklyn and Staten Island) producing a contaminated "dead sea." The shoreward movement of this waste now threatens the Atlantic beaches along Long Island and Staten Island with contamination and closure. Also threatened, by way of the long shore currents, is the multimillion dollar resort industry of the New Jersey shore north of Atlantic City.

AIR POLLUTION

If New York is threatening the pollution of the New Jersey shore by water, New Jersey is striking back by air. The prevailing westerly winds bring the pollutants from refineries, chemical plants, industries, and cities like Newark and Jersey City over the Hudson River to mingle with the pollution dome generated by New York. The result is a pollution layer which is unmatched by any other major American metropolitan region.

Fundamentally, there are two kinds of pollution—oxidizing and reducing. The reducing type was typical of the nineteenth century industrial city. The burning of fossil fuels often releases into the air chemicals such as sulphur dioxide which, upon contact with atmospheric moisture, become acidic—in this case, sulfuric acid. The chemical action of such materials is searing, burning, and irritating to exposed tissue surfaces. The oxidizing type of pollution—also

Figure 44. Tidal Marshland, New Jersey Meadowlands. Grading and bulldozing (foreground), salt hay meadows (middle distance), light industrial–warehousing complex (background). Pollution destroyed much of the fishing-hunting-recreational ecology which prevailed in this area at the turn of the century. Landfill and development is proceeding on the carcass.

called photochemical smog—results when a complex of petroleum-derived organic chemicals mixes in the air in the presence of sunlight. The end product of these reactions is chemical ozone, which also has a corrosive effect on tissues. Vapors from burning gasoline and the New Jersey refineries are rich sources of these chemicals.

The two types of pollution are antagonistic to each other. Thus, when reducing pollution dominates, the photochemical reactions are arrested and oxidizing pollution disappears. New York has both.

In the winter, the New Yorker may experience old fashioned reducing pollution arising from the burning of fossil fuels for power and heat. In the summer, when these sources subside, photochemical smog takes over to assail the lungs and nostrils of the public. On a clear day in spring or summer, the dust dome over the region is clearly visible from the New Jersey Turnpike as the traveler looks toward the New York City skyline.

SOLID WASTE DISPOSAL—LANDFILL AND THE GROWTH OF NEW YORK

New York City is no stranger to the landfill process. About one-third of Manhattan is filled or reclaimed land. As long ago as the seventeenth and eighteenth centuries, a more or less spontaneous fill process was underway. Water Street—several blocks inland in southern Manhattan—once approximately marked the shoreline. Piers projected into the East River, and sewage poured down gutter trenches into the slips which lay between the piers. As a slip filled in above the low tide line, the foul odors prompted the residents to lay dirt above it, filling in the slip, and then extending new piers out still further. It is a matter inviting ironic reflection that some of the most expensive land in the world (near Wall Street) is basically formed of antique sanitary wastes. Also, every street west of Tenth Avenue and south of 59th Street is composed of landfill. More recently, projects have been initiated in the downtown area to develop landfill sites to accommodate a new home for the Stock Exchange, and to develop a PUD "new town in town" near Battery Park overlooking the harbor vista.

Landfill has also accounted for the development of Port Newark–Port Elizabeth, and many an unsuspecting city resident lives upon a tract which was once a garbage dump. But landfill sites are now scarce. Barging incinerated wastes out to the New York Bight sludge area is becoming more and more common as an alternative to the incredible landscape of trash in northwestern Staten Island.

Almost every major city has an area of automobile graveyards, scrapyards, and the like, often along blighted water courses where barge traffic is available or in poorly drained land where normal development has been slow. The tidal marsh area known as the Jersey Meadows northeast of Newark is typical. To a certain extent they serve a useful purpose as dumps, especially for wrecked automobiles, which formerly were widely abandoned in the streets of many cities until scrap prices rose high enough to pay for their collection.

As garbage and refuse disposal becomes an increasing need in metropolitan areas, sites suitable for these uses become scarcer and open incineration becomes prevalent. Since open dumping provides an optimum breeding environment for rats and other vermin, sanitary landfill dumps are often sought, where every day's load of refuse has some six inches of dirt bulldozed over it. Unfortunately this method, which is relatively inexpensive $4.50 to $5 per ton, 1974 prices), is an extensive user of land. On the average, one acre of land is required for each 10,000 people, and may only be used for about five years. Clearly, a city of a million would need one hundred acres every five years, and between the growth in urban demand and the decreasing supply of land, this method is most suited to the relatively less densely settled suburb, and even there is of limited use. By 1963, several Westchester towns were trucking garbage sixty miles to landfill sites, while the same suburban New York county in 1967 was considering exporting its garbage 200 miles upstate at night by rail, since the nearer landfill sites were exhausted. At the same time, San Francisco was considering a 450 mile rail haul for its garbage.

Tragically, the potential of composting, recycling, and other constructive alternatives to sanitary landfill methods have barely been considered in the region. At Howland's Hook in northern Staten Island, looking across the land polluted with garbage toward the septic Arthur Kill and the Kill van Kull, where the sediment washed from the garbage flats into the water is deposited along with the material from the outfalls from the New Jersey chemical plants, one can easily see the industrial smoke stacks poisoning the air. It is a domain of seagulls and rats.

Conclusion

Like many other American metropolitan areas, the NYMR is experiencing the suburbanization of human activities. Jobs in manufacturing, transportation, wholesaling, retailing, and various services (including some like finance, insurance, and real estate which traditionally have been centralized) have migrated out into the suburban perimeters of the old core cities like New York, Newark, Paterson, Jersey City, and Bridgeport. Of course, it has been even more true that the recent past has witnessed the strong decentralization of residence in the region.

Economically, what this amounts to is a disinvestment in the city accompanied by investment in perimeter areas. Hughes and James have reviewed some of the forces which are driving this process forward in the NYMR. Space needs have generated a demand for large-sized building lots for modern plants which are difficult to secure in core city locations where land values are high and land parcels are small. Related to this are the increased needs for loading and unloading aprons for trucks and railcars, along with warehousing facility needs.

Simultaneously, innovations in transportation and communications technology have freed many factories from a dependence upon rail or water access. Furthermore, within many firms it is no longer necessary for head office functions to be located at the site of production, since data-processing systems and communications links allow control to be exercised from some distance.

The classic economic raison de'etre for the existence of a city—the economic gain which may be realized by using the nearby independent business and financial services which abound in the city external to the firm itself—is now increasingly neutralized by the fact that suburbanization of enterprise has made these external economies available in the suburbs.

Trends in automation and technological development tend to shift hiring needs of firms from many unskilled workers to fewer skilled workers. The imperative to locate the plant near a massive manpower pool is thus eased, while the weakness of unions in the NYMR suburbs (as compared to the city) may be attractive to some firms. The suburbs also provide a strengthening white collar labor pool compared to the city.

The prestige and image of a firm is related to its location. As the prestigious New York City address is perceived as tarnished by the negative attributes which have become identified with old core citites (often unjustly, as figures on violent crime in New York City compared with other cities and with suburban crime increases show), the firm's image may be buttressed by a more sylvan location, preferably visible from a parkway.

But in addition to all of these points, Hughes and James suggest that a very important consideration in the decision to locate in the suburbs is tied to the upbringing of today's young executives. A generation of young corporate managers was reared in the suburbs. Unlike preceding generations of executives who might recall with fondness their city childhood, these young adults have had little or no exposure to the city, except as a location from which their family fled. For them, the suburb is the norm, the city terra incognita.

All these forces have helped to decentralize NYMR business and residential activity, while the balkanization of political jurisdiction in the region has been incapable of resisting the tide. Perhaps as the 1970s advance and ominous trends toward a continuing energy crisis and recession in the building and construction trades mature, the time will ripen for the reestablishment of city life which remains relatively more economical of materials and energy than the suburban-style single family house cum automobile. In my opinion, however, this time is still relatively remote, at least in the NYMR.

The newest suburbs around the old cities of the NYMR tend to be developed as complete and relatively efficient land use packages rather than the stereotype of a single purpose residential subdivision. Shopping center, office tower, industrial park, multiple dwelling, and single family residence are all woven into the fabric. Even the shopping center, which has been stigmatized by some as the destroyer of the urban texture provided by the central business district, has been broadening its functional base to include some of those amenities as the functional bases of many downtowns have been eroding. In some suburban malls in the NYMR, noncommercial activities like churches and community meeting halls have been incorporated, extending both the social utility and the use time of the mall into evening and weekend activities and thus improving its efficiency.

The social function of the suburban activity center has spilled over from a narrow retailing purpose into broader social purposes. Senior citizens frequent the enclosed malls, taking advantage of controlled climates and safety-patrolled corridors. Teenagers come to the malls for dating and social life. In fact, the *paseo* characteristic of the central square of a Latin American small town, a time of ritualized strolling on the part of young men and women for the purpose of socializing, resembles the social pattern of the suburban shopping center. In the one case the town hall and the church are the two ceremonial terminals of the interaction space, while in the other case they are two major retailing institutions. In both cases

the sides of the space tend to be lined by shops, and the central space public, well lighted, well patrolled, and safe.

In our opinion these suburban activity foci of the NYMR are evolving toward the form of an enclosed minicity in which social functions proceed in an atmosphere of relaxation, comfort, and safety. They are now well on the way to becoming the critical points of intersection of a growing suburban public transportation system.

And what of the central cities? Mayor Kenneth Gibson of Newark is supposed to have remarked that while he didn't know where American cities were going, he believed that Newark would get there first. The comment must be interpreted with some pessimism since, in fact, those with the financial options seem to be vacating Newark as fast as they can. Prime, modern office towers in a downtown area that is still regionally second only to Manhattan in terms of financial institutions are plagued with unfillable vacancies as the city struggles against decline. The central ward, afflicted with a poverty population and declining housing stock, manifests high abandonment rates and high municipal service needs.

As Newark becomes a city of municipal services provided to a poor population without an adequate tax base, the Newark worker is faced with the rising costs of commuting to the perimeter suburban factory belt coupled with a rising tax rate. In the case of Newark (and perhaps elsewhere) these tendencies cut across racial and ethnic groups. The middle class Newark black is moving to the suburbs along with middle class whites. The residuum in the city includes the poor of all groups. Of course, owing to the discriminatory practices of our economic system, blacks and Hispanics are disproportionately represented among Newark's poor, but the central city–suburban dichotomy is becoming more class based and less based on race or ethnicity as time goes on.

What we are suggesting here is that the benefits and costs of the NYMR are increasingly concentrating in geographically separated areas. Benefits, and the principal beneficiaries, are concentrating around the suburban "minicities" which are thought of as safe and of a desirable human scale, while social costs and the residences of the poor are cordoned off into central city "cost sinks." In some instances, as economic functions vacate central city office structures, government offices become "renters of last resort." Much of the World Trade Center and many other downtown office sites in Manhattan are thus increasingly occupied by state and federal functions. In Norton Long's metaphor, the city becomes a reservation for the poor and public sector institutions to which service-providing custodians commute. The urban enrichment of the circumcity zone accompanies the impoverishment of the center.

It is our view that, in the short term, there seems little prospect that these trends will alter in the NYMR. As political power follows economic power to the numerous small suburban jurisdictions it seems unlikely that they will act in a way to force the redistribution of resources on an intra-state basis to the few large central city jurisdictions, most especially in a national climate of receding economic indicators. Similarly, a national government which has turned away from the concept of strong federal intervention in local affairs on behalf of the cities is unlikely to force a redistribution of resources to central cities equal to the task of deflecting these tendencies, even if its political constituency would tolerate it. Insofar as court decisions can achieve resource redistribution, recent judicial actions have indeed forced piecemeal, spotty remedies for inequitable funding of public programs—in housing, public sanitation, and education, for example. But it is not within the court's power to initiate the kind of massive effort that the renewal of Newark would require.

Finally, it must be observed that the "minicity" lifestyle which is developing in the suburban reaches of the NYMR is probably preferred by the overwhelming majority of regional residents including, and even especially, those who are trapped in the old cities. To a great extent, the regret of many of them seems to be less that the center city is declining than that they lack the means to leave it, and are forced to reside in a landscape of despair.

Bibliography

Albion, Robert G. *The Rise of New York Port: 1815-1860*. New York, 1939.

Asbury, Herbert. *The Gangs of New York*. New York, 1927.

Bryson, R.A., and J.E. Kutzbach. *Air Pollution*. Resource Paper no. 2. Washington, D.C.: Association of American Geographers, Commission on College Geography, 1968.

Burchell, Robert W., with James W. Hughes. *Planned Units Development*. Rutgers University, New Brunswick, N.J.: Center for Urban Policy Research, 1973.

Carey, George W.; Leonard Zobler; Michael R. Greenberg; and Robert M. Hordon. *Urbanization, Water Pollution, and Public Policy*. New Brunswick, N.J.: Rutgers University, Center for Urban Policy Research, 1973.

Deutsch, Karl W. "On Social Communication and the Metropolis." *General Systems Yearbook* VI (1961): 95-100.

Dubois, W.E.B. *The Philadelphia Negro*. New York: Shocken Books, originally published 1899.

Duffy, J. *A History of Public Health in New York City, 1625-1866*. New York: Russel Sage Foundation, 1968.

Gottmann, Jean. *Megalopolis: The Urbanized Northeastern Seaboard of the U.S.* New York, 1961.

Gustafson, W. Eric. "Printing and Publishing." In Max Hall, ed., *Made in New York*, ch. 2. Cambridge, Mass.: Harvard University Press, 1959.

Hall, Max, ed. *Made in New York*. New York Metropolitan Regional Study. Cambridge, Mass.: Harvard University Press, 1959.

Handlin, Oscar. *The Newcomers*. New York Metropolitan Regional Study. Cambridge, Mass.: Harvard University Press, 1959.

Helfgott, Roy B. "Women's and Children's Apparel." In Max Hall, ed., *Made in New York*, ch. 1. Cambridge, Mass.: Harvard University Press, 1959.

Hoover, Edgar M., and Raymond Vernon. *Anatomy of a Metropolis*, Cambridge, Mass.: Harvard University Press, 1959.

Hughes, James, and Franklin J. James. "Suburbanization Dynamics and the Transportation Dillimma." In James Hughes and Franklin J. James, eds., *Suburbanization Dynamics and the Future of the City*, pp. 19-42. New Brunswick, N.J.: Rutgers University, Center for Urban Policy Research, 1974.

Huxtable, Ada Louise. *Classic New York*. New York: Doubleday and Company, Anchor Books 1964.

Jacobs, Jane, *The Death and Life of Great American Cities*, Vintage Books, Random House, N.Y., 1961, page 270 ff.

Jonassen, Christen T. "Cultural Variables in the Ecology of an Ethnic Group." *American Sociological Review* 14 (February, 1949): 32-41.

Kenyon, James B. *Industrial Location and Metropolitan Growth, the Paterson-Passaic District*. Chicago: University of Chicago Department of Geography, Research Paper no. 67, 1960.

Long, Norton. "The City as Reservation." *The Public Interest* 25 (Fall 1971): 3-14.

McDermott, W. "Air Pollution and Public Health." *Scientific American*, October 1961.

Osofsky, Gilbert. *Harlem: The Making of a Ghetto.* New York: Harper and Row, 1966.

Port Authority of New York and New Jersey. *Port Authority Handbook.* New York, 1973.

Regional Plan Association. *Regional Survey of New York and its Environs.* New York, 1929.

Riis, Jacob A. *How the Other Half Lives: Studies Among the Tenements of New York, 1919.* New York, 1919. Reprinted Harvard U. Press 1970.

Rischin, Moses. *The Promised City: New York's Jews, 1870–1914.* Cambridge, 1962.

Robbins, Sidney M., and Nestor E. Terleckyj. *Money Metropolis.* New York Metropolitan Regional Study. Cambridge, Mass.: Harvard University Press, 1960.

Samuelson, Paul. *Economics.* 7th ed., pp. 12 and 13. New York: McGraw-Hill, 1965.

Sternlieb, George. *The Tenement Landlord.* New Brunswick, N.J.: Rutgers University Press, 1969.

———. *The Urban Housing Dilemma.* New York: The Housing and Development Administration of the City of New York, Department of Rent and Housing Maintenance, Office of Rent Control, 1972.

Sternlieb, George, and Robert W. Burchell. *Residential Abandonment, the Tenement Landlord Revisited.* Center for Urban Policy Research, New Brunswick, N.J.: Rutgers University, 1973.

Sternlieb, George, and James W. Hughes. *Housing and People in New York City.* New York: The Housing and Development Administration of the City of New York, Department of Rent and Housing Maintenance, 1973.

U.S. Department of Commerce. *The Automobile and Air Pollution: A Program for Progress.* Report of the Panel on Electrically Powered Vehicles. Washington, D.C., 1967.

Ware, Caroline F. *Greenwich Village: 1920–1930.* Boston, 1935.

Warntz, William. *Macrogeography and Income Fronts.* Regional Science Research Institute Monograph 3. Philadelphia, 1965.

Weber, Adna F. *The Growth of Cities in the Nineteenth Century.* Vol. XI, Columbia University Studies in History, Economics, and Public Law. 1899.

White, Norval, and Elliot Wilensky. *The American Institute of Architects (AIA) Guide to New York City.* New York: MacMillan Company, 1968.

Wood, Robert. *1400 Government.* Cambridge, Mass: Harvard Univ. Press. 1961.

Works Progress Administration, Federal Workers' Project. *New York City Guide.* New York: Random House, 1939.

About the Author

Dr. George W. Carey, who is Professor of Urban Planning and Public Administration in the Department of Urban Studies at Rutgers University (Newark) was trained in geography and has done extensive research in the New York Metropolitan Region on ecologically-oriented topics relating such things as water pollution, water supply, and land use with regional changes in socioeconomic patterns. Much of his work has involved the design of mathematical models with public policy implications.